PRAISE FOR
SAFE DANGER

"Our story about risk is getting in the way of creating the future we need. Ben opens the door for teams to come alive, wake up, and make an impact."

—Seth Godin, best-selling author of *This Is Strategy* and *This Is Marketing*

"Delightful and profound, *Safe Danger* delivers on its provocative title. Author Ben Swire offers a timeless guide to live a fuller and more innovative life and become a better leader. With its engaging stories and practical creative activities, this may be one of the most useful management books you will read this year."

—Amy C. Edmondson, Novartis Professor of Leadership at Harvard Business School, author of *Right Kind of Wrong: The Science of Failing Well*, and the person whose work brought the term "psychological safety" into everyday life.

"*Safe Danger* is a blueprint for building cultures where connection and creativity become the norm—not the exception. With the insight of a designer and the heart of a humanist, Ben Swire shows how small risks can lead to big breakthroughs—in teams, in culture, and in ourselves."

—Tim Brown, author of *Change by Design* and chair of IDEO

"I didn't expect a book about risk to be so fun. But I guess that's exactly the point! *Safe Danger* doesn't just lay out the facts and tell you why taking small risks matters—it actually gives you an experience and makes you feel it."

—Jad Abumrad, Peabody Award-winning creator of *Radiolab*, *More Perfect*, and *Dolly Parton's America*

"*Safe Danger* is about more than team building; it is about the invisible forces that shape our relationships, our creativity, and our very sense of belonging. Swire is a brilliant guide and reminds us that risk is not just the domain of thrill seekers or disruptors but is woven into the fabric of human connection. Through small, playful, and intentional acts of courage, we can transform not just our teams but also ourselves."

—Jordan Harbinger, host of *The Jordan Harbinger Show*

"*Safe Danger* is a powerful exploration of the paradoxes that make us human—our craving for safety and our longing for aliveness. With heart, depth, and practical wisdom, this book invites us to expand our comfort zones—not by abandoning security but by redefining it. A must-read for anyone seeking to grow beyond their fears and also looking for tools that will actually help make it happen."

—Dr. Scott Barry Kaufman, host of *The Psychology Podcast* and best-selling author of *Transcend*

"Calling all reluctant heroes...Ben Swire's book, *Safe Danger*, is an amazing combination of fantastic storytelling, useful advice, and has an authentic practical application element for any leader who strives to build a great team. It will be useful for leaders in a wide variety of fields—from Fortune 100 companies, sports teams, and entrepreneurs—to lead creative people. It's well done and useful. Buy this, read it, and apply it. Your future self will thank you."

—Ryan Hawk, host of *The Learning Leader Show* and author of *Welcome to Management*, *The Pursuit of Excellence*, and *The Score That Matters*

"There are no two better words to describe brilliant team cultures than *Safe Danger*. Ben Swire has captured the essence of what makes great teams great, effective leaders beloved, and innovative companies soar. There are no platitudes—just hard and fast advice born from the front lines of creative work."

—Todd Henry, host of the *Daily Creative* podcast and author of *The Accidental Creative* and *Herding Tigers*

"A must-read for any human at work. With a mix of humor, psychology, and real-world exercises, this warm and witty book teaches you how to take small, fun, and manageable risks that help you build trust, unlock creativity, and reconnect with what excites you."

—Mollie West Duffy, best-selling coauthor of *No Hard Feelings: The Secret Power of Embracing Emotions at Work*

"*Safe Danger* shows us how to use strategic play to power both our professional and personal endeavors. Swire has gifted the playbook for how to collaborate with others to do the best work of your life."

—Ryder Carroll, creator of the *Bullet Journal* method

"If I know anything, it is that people can only do their best work when they are connected and trust each other. *Safe Danger* takes what we dismiss as 'just fun' and reveals it as the secret to deep, lasting connection. For those who understand the power of play, Ben Swire has delivered a gift. Leaders who want to cultivate impactful, thriving teams need to get their hands on this book!"

—Megan Summers, global head of production at Facebook

"The world doesn't need another book about innovation, but it does need this one. Ben's take is refreshing, logical, and eye-opening."

—Clayton Ruebensaal, chief creative officer at Comcast

"*Safe Danger* is a practical road map to navigate the emotional fundamentals that lead to workplace transformation. With a mix of playful challenges and sharp insights, Ben Swire shows how small, low-stakes risks can build real trust, unlock creativity, and help teams actually connect—not just pretend to. It's not just smart; it's very doable and refreshingly human."

—Victoria Lubomski, senior director of human resources and global business services at Boston Consulting Group

"Creativity blooms when risk and play hold hands. Ben Swire reveals that when we dive joyfully into the things we're most uncertain about, we can forge deeper connections, ignite fresh ideas, and make surprising discoveries. In *Safe Danger*, Ben shows us how."   —Alex Gallafent, executive director at IDEO

"As an educator, I've grown wary of the term 'safe spaces'—especially when what many students really need is a space to engage with dangerous ideas. But true dialogue doesn't begin with risk. It starts with trust. *Safe Danger* offers a thoughtful, practical approach to build the psychological safety that allows curiosity, connection, and even productive disagreement to flourish. Through creative exercises and compelling storytelling, Ben Swire provides an essential tool kit for anyone looking to spark meaningful growth in their team, classroom, or community."

—Eli Woolery, lecturer in the Design Program at Stanford University and cohost of the *Design Better* podcast

"A must-read for anyone who is tired of playing it safe but also afraid to shake things up. *Safe Danger* is a beautiful, practical guide to practice courage in small, meaningful ways. In a world that often demands we stay polished and protected, Ben Swire makes the case for something wilder and more alive—small, playful risks that help us build trust, unlock creativity, and reconnect with what excites us. With wit, wisdom, and a generous spirit, he offers real-world tools for anyone—leaders, creatives, and teams alike—ready to do brave, transformative work. Read it, use it, and watch your team—and yourself—transform."

—Andrea Stangarone, director of design operations at Yahoo!

"Ben Swire is one of the most thoughtful and creative minds I have had the chance to work with—brilliant, disarming, and endlessly curious. In *Safe Danger*, he captures something quietly radical: The idea that the smallest risks—when approached with care and play—can spark the deepest connections. This book is part tool kit, part manifesto, and entirely heart. It's a gift to anyone who wants to build trust, fuel purpose, and do work that actually matters. I've seen Ben's methods in action—and I can say from experience that they truly work."

—Matthew Hassett, founder and CEO of Loftie

SAFE DANGER

BEN SWIRE

SAFE DANGER

An Unexpected Method for Sparking
Connection, Finding Purpose,
and Inspiring Innovation

balance

New York Boston

Copyright © 2025 by Benjamin Swire
Illustrations by cartoonist Juan Astasio of *The New Yorker*
Cover images © Shutterstock

Cover copyright © 2025 by Hachette Book Group, Inc.

Hachette Book Group supports the right to free expression and the value of copyright. The purpose of copyright is to encourage writers and artists to produce the creative works that enrich our culture.

The scanning, uploading, and distribution of this book without permission is a theft of the author's intellectual property. If you would like permission to use material from the book (other than for review purposes), please contact Permissions@hbgusa.com. Thank you for your support of the author's rights.

Balance
Hachette Book Group
1290 Avenue of the Americas
New York, NY 10104
GCP-Balance.com
@GCPBalance

First Edition: October 2025

Balance is an imprint of Grand Central Publishing. The Balance name and logo are registered trademarks of Hachette Book Group, Inc.

The publisher is not responsible for websites (or their content) that are not owned by the publisher.

The Hachette Speakers Bureau provides a wide range of authors for speaking events. To find out more, visit hachettespeakersbureau.com or email HachetteSpeakers@hbgusa.com.

Balance books may be purchased in bulk for business, educational, or promotional use. For information, please contact your local bookseller or email the Hachette Book Group Special Markets Department at Special.Markets@hbgusa.com.

Print book interior design by Amy Quinn

Library of Congress Cataloging-in-Publication Data

Name: Swire, Ben author
Title: Safe danger: an unexpected method for sparking connection, finding purpose, and inspiring innovation / Ben Swire.
Description: First edition. | New York: Balance, 2025. | Includes bibliographical references.
Identifiers: LCCN 2025017090 | ISBN 9780306833823 hardcover | ISBN 9780306833830 trade paperback | ISBN 9780306833847 ebook
Subjects: LCSH: Risk-taking (Psychology) | Self-actualization (Psychology)
Classification: LCC BF637.R57 S95 2025 | DDC 155.9—dc23/eng/20250718
LC record available at https://lccn.loc.gov/2025017090

ISBNs: 978-0-306-83382-3 (hardcover); 978-0-306-83384-7 (ebook)

Printed in the United States of America

LSC-C

Printing 1, 2025

CONTENTS

Introduction — *xi*

Part I
TO SPARK CHANGE, FUEL SAFE DANGER

CHAPTER ONE
Safe Danger — 3
Activity: Super Secret — *16*

CHAPTER TWO
Safety That Sparks Instead of Stagnates — 27
Activity: Moving Stories — *31*

CHAPTER THREE
Danger That Thrills Instead of Threatens — 39

Part II
TO BOOST QUALITY, FOCUS ON QUALITIES

CHAPTER FOUR
To Accelerate Productivity, Inspire Joy — 53
Activity: Hidden Joys — *70*

CHAPTER FIVE
To Pinpoint Purpose, Inspire Vulnerability — 77
Activity: Homegrown Heroes — *93*

CHAPTER SIX
To Energize Bold Thinking, Inspire Curiosity — 101
Activity: Mash-Up Mindset — *114*

CHAPTER SEVEN
To Foster Resilience, Inspire Optimism   121
Activity: Unblinking Line   *126*

CHAPTER EIGHT
To Fuel Collaboration, Inspire Connection   143
Activity: Emblemottos   *147*

CHAPTER NINE
To Build Community, Inspire Trust   161
Activity: Skin in the Game   *165*

CHAPTER TEN
To Prepare for the Unknown, Inspire Creativity   177

Part III
MORE ACTIVITIES OF SAFE DANGER

CHAPTER ELEVEN
Facilitation   189

CHAPTER TWELVE
The Activities   199

Acknowledgments   *255*
Notes   *257*
About the Author   *265*

INTRODUCTION

BUT FIRST, A SECRET

Before we begin, I need to risk telling you something. It may sound like exactly the wrong thing for the author of a book about creative activities to admit, but it's the truth and I think it's important to be honest about it: I would never have gone to one of my own workshops. Not voluntarily. I'm an introvert's introvert and have never been one for group activities. I would rather gnaw off a limb than do another skit at an offsite. Party games make me run for the hills. Karaoke gives me the heebie-jeebies.

But here's the thing: I would have been missing out. I know this because whenever I roped people into coming to my sessions for the first time, they left saying things like, "You know, I actually really, really enjoyed that." And though that was, of course, the polite response to give, I know that they meant it because I never had to rope them in again. They came back on their own. They made time, brought their clients, invited friends. They published articles about the workshops. They said the sessions were one of the defining highlights of our community's culture. So, yeah, I would have been missing out.

This book is less about convincing you to try something new and more about sharing what convinced me. I'm hoping it will make it easier to understand the people you spend your days with and to be understood by them. I'm hoping it will help you pinpoint what you have to say, why it's worth the risk to say it, and how to shout it from the rooftops with confidence.

CALLING ALL RELUCTANT HEROES

Ask people what they want most out of life and you'll likely hear: *inspiring experiences, exciting work, meaningful relationships,* and *making a difference.* But ask how they're doing on that wish list and, more often than not, it's still just that: a wish list.

Big goals like those require big risks like trusting others and inviting disappointment. As a result, we end up with a chasm between what we want and what we're willing to do to get it.

You've probably heard of the hero's journey.

Once upon a time, there was a hero who didn't know they were a hero. There was a crisis, and though the hero clung to the safe and familiar, they had no choice but to set out on the adventure. The hero met friends who helped and faced challenges that hindered, until finally the hero came face-to-face with the thing they least wanted to face. It didn't look good for the hero until they were finally able to draw on hitherto unseen inner resources to emerge victorious, in possession of a reward of great value. They returned to their life, forever changed.

Dorothy in Oz? Frodo in Middle Earth? Simba in the pride lands? You in middle school? This, in a nutshell, is the hero's journey as laid out by Joseph Campbell in his brilliant book *The Hero with a Thousand Faces*. Campbell mapped out the beats of classic stories from around the world and found this consistent pattern across humanity's stories, myths, and fables.

The beats of the hero's journey are generally as follows:

Call to Adventure	The Innermost Cave
Refusal of the Call	The Ordeal
Meeting the Mentor	Seizing the Reward
Crossing the Threshold	Resurrection
Tests, Allies, Enemies	Return to the Ordinary World

You can spot the hero's journey everywhere, from the *Odyssey* to *Legally Blonde*. But for Campbell this is about more than just good story structure. This is about life. This is wisdom. He believed that the stories we tell ourselves as a species are more than entertainment; they're repositories of insight and truth to be absorbed, learned from, and put into practice. They're how we teach ourselves about being human. For Campbell, these stories were telling us that the rewards we seek will not be easy pickings, that our greatest enemy and our secret strength can both be found within, that nothing of value comes without sacrifice and struggle, but that this is how we grow and improve both ourselves and the world around us.

For many of us, adventure may look less like lightsabers and magic beans and more like an opportunity to try something new, defend what we believe in, or take a different path than the one handed to us. But most of us don't hear the call as adventure—we hear it as risk. As danger.

A key part of Campbell's hero's journey is the hero's response to the call to adventure: "No thanks." The hero is reluctant. Why? Because they're scared! They're afraid of failing. They're afraid of change. People aren't risk-takers in general. The *real* risk-takers were weeded out of our bloodlines by those sabertooth tigers eons ago. So the stories we tell ourselves give the same advice: Be courageous, take a risk, it'll be worth it. We keep telling ourselves the hero's journey in all its various forms because we need the encouragement.

Risk is scary, but deep down we know it's the only way to grow. Becoming something new means leaving behind the old. No one ever sailed to a new land without losing sight of the familiar shore. If we want to grow, we need to find the courage to walk into danger.

"But what if something goes <u>right</u>?"

To do this, we need a way to make those risks feel less dangerous, more worthwhile, and, frankly, more fun.

That is where this book comes in.

SAFE DANGER'S ORIGIN STORY

The most pivotal transition of my career came when I left my role as a VP of Marketing at a blue-chip financial institution to join IDEO, the iconic design and innovation firm. I'd known lovely people in the financial marketing world. We laughed, enjoyed each other's company, and I thought that was as good as I should expect from work. I was wrong. Moving to IDEO was like stepping from Kansas into Oz. A whole Technicolor spectrum of possibilities suddenly flooded in.

IDEO had a culture that valued both joy and rigor, both bravery and vulnerability, both the head and the heart. It was a random group of people with distinct backgrounds, goals, and interests, and yet it was a community that valued and explored those distinctions. It was a place where people enjoyed staying late to help out on other people's projects. In fact, one of the first things I noticed was the difference in how the corporate world and IDEO viewed asking for help. People are often hesitant to ask for help at work because it's seen as evidence they can't do their job, places them lower in the hierarchy of internal politics, and imposes on other people who are already overworked. At IDEO, asking for help was seen as the highest form of flattery. If you went to someone for their expertise, it wasn't a burden but a sign of respect and admiration and an opportunity for that person to add some of their value to make the work better.

All that said, IDEO was also an intense and demanding place. Even though we were all aware of the importance of refilling our own creative wells after giving so much to the work, as is often the case, self-care consistently fell to the bottom of the to-do list.

To help refuel and refresh our community, I designed a series of biweekly events I called creative playdates. Part team building, part speed dating, part imaginative experiment, they used deceptively simple, but carefully designed creative activities to help us stay inspired, understand each other better, and practice tricky things like vulnerability and trust that we needed to do our best work.

Over time we started using the activities with clients, and I eventually spun them off into their own offer. I'll be honest. One of the big question marks for me when I took these activities beyond the walls of IDEO was, Would it work? IDEO was a self-selecting group of people committed to curiosity and willing to take time to play. But what about the rest of the world? The serious world? Would accountants play with googly eyes? Would analysts enjoy making music with found objects? Doubtful.

Boy, was I wrong.

In the years since I first began designing my activities, I've led workshops for organizations ranging from Fortune 500 stalwarts to first year start-ups. I've hosted them for parties, workplaces, and communities. I've run them virtually, in-person, and various mish-moshes of the two. I've seen firsthand how they can invigorate individuals, build bonds between colleagues, and reignite stagnating team spirits. Engineers, lawyers, good friends, utter strangers. Eight-year-olds and eighty-year-olds.

I've found that creative activities that provide what I call "safe danger" are the perfect tool to build productivity, purpose, bold thinking, resilience, collaboration, and community and to prepare for the unknowns around the corner. Essentially, I use creative play to make the scary stuff more manageable. I think of creativity like oven mitts: It's a safe way to handle dangerous material. My activities are not for learning about art; they're for learning about each other *through* art. Empathy, not artistry. I'm not asking for talent, I'm asking for intention. If you show up to these activities with kindness, curiosity, and generosity, you'll knock it out of the park, regardless of whether your artwork looks more like Lisa Simpson than the *Mona Lisa*.

Safe danger isn't about unleashing creativity. It's about unleashing you.

Over the years I've come to see that people who risk embracing seven specific qualities consistently bring out the best behaviors, most exciting connections, and most unique ideas from themselves, their teams, and their families: joy, vulnerability, curiosity, optimism, connection, trust, and creativity. The problem is the dynamics of those qualities can be surprisingly hard to understand for the very simple reason that most of us think we already do.

We don't.

At least, not as much as we think we do. That's because understanding these qualities requires more than an intellectual understanding; they require experiential understanding. They require practice. But practicing them is tough because (1) most of us are not so great about regularly practicing stuff we think we already know and (2) these are traits that require a commitment to be meaningful.

Safe danger is how I get around those obstacles. Safe danger helps us truly experience, practice, and understand these qualities in a way that can change the choices we make and the lives we lead.

Most people are living someone else's life. They're following other people's rules and achieving other people's goals. The problem starts when we lose what makes us stand out. But it's not just that we lose these unique parts of ourselves—we learn early on to actively hide them. Sometimes these things are significant, other times they're more subtle, but inevitably we end up locking away some of what makes us different, makes our perspective unique, makes us *us*. Brené Brown has a wonderful take on the difference between belonging and fitting in: "Fitting in is about assessing a situation and becoming who you need to be to be accepted. Belonging, on the other hand, doesn't require us to change who we are; it requires us to be who we are." Emotionally, fitting in is the opposite of belonging.

For grown-ups, the problem is that many of us, quite frankly, have forgotten who we are. (If, that is, we ever gave ourselves permission to be ourselves in the first place.)

"Listen to me, son—if you believe in yourself, keep your head down, and work really hard, you can make all my dreams come true."

Most of us, most of the time, are conditioned to fit in. School, work, home, family, society, and friends all teach us how to behave like everyone else, to conform. Because, you know, we live in a society. Sometimes that's just fine. I wouldn't be thrilled to sip coffee in a café next to someone clipping their toenails. But, while blending in may seem like the smart move to survive middle school, it can leave our light diminished for the rest of our lives.

This book is about how to rekindle that light. It's full of easy, fun activities built around the sort of risks that will help you find meaning and purpose for yourself, be more productive and effective, and feel more joyful and confident in your own skin. Because if you're not speaking with your own unique voice, if you're living the life you were told to live instead of the one you were meant to live, the world is missing out. The people who mean the most to you, the people who look up to you, and many, many people you may never even meet, they're all missing out if you're not standing out.

HOW TO USE THIS BOOK

I've found that most books like this focus on one of two audiences: people trying to be more successful in business, or people trying to be more successful in their regular life. Business or personal. I don't believe this is a healthy distinction.

Because most people carry their workday into their home life and their home life into their workday, my approach is to dissolve the distinction between the two as much as possible without sacrificing the value of the insights. The personal is the professional is the personal.

Whether you are a leader looking to engage your team, a professional looking to infuse your career with new life, or a person looking to get more out of your time on earth, there's a lot in this book that will help regardless of who it seems to be addressed to. In fact, the parts that seem least targeted to your particular context may be the most helpful.

Building a strong team is about understanding what each person has to contribute and clearing a path so that they can contribute fully. So is raising a family. Finding your own unique voice in the world is about clearing away your fears to see the value you have to contribute. So is growing a healthy relationship. Our personal and professional lives exist in distinct arenas, but what is valuable to one is often just as valuable to the other, even though we may not see it at first. Regardless of which shelf you pulled this book from, every chapter can be about you, or about your team, or about your family, or about your friends, or about your community. It just depends on where you choose to use it. So take what you like and leave the rest.

Part I focuses on the what. What are we talking about when we talk safety, when we talk danger, and when we combine them. Part II is about the why. Each chapter focuses on one of the seven powerful qualities I mentioned above and why it's so impactful to unlock it with safe danger. Part III is the how. It contains instructions for my activities and a guide for how to facilitate them.

Emotional risk-taking is not something you learn; it's something you practice. So each chapter also describes a group activity that can be used with coworkers, family, friends, or a shared community. But I know perfectly well that we're not all going to be hosting crafting parties every night. So, though I love and believe in all the creative group activities I'll be sharing, I've also collected some solo exercises from creatives and professionals who have found simple, low-lift ways to infuse their lives with the qualities discussed in each chapter. These "Habit Builders" are small, everyday nudges that you can practice and use right away to help break some of those mental behaviors that stand in your way.

A nice aspect of the safe danger activities is that they are actually pretty simple. Although they are infused with elements of art interpretation, crafting hour, therapy, team dynamics, esoterica, storytelling, daydreaming, puzzles, and the hero's journey beneath the surface, none of these elements takes center stage—in the moment, the activities are simply fun. They are designed to be playful, but purposeful; to work around a conference table or a dinner table; to connect new colleagues or old college friends. However you chose to use them, they are designed to be worth your time.

Whether your goal is to enrich the path you're on or to find a new one to explore, safe danger is the missing piece you've been looking for.

**SAFE
DANGER**

PART I

TO SPARK CHANGE, FUEL SAFE DANGER

CHAPTER ONE

SAFE DANGER

HERE'S A SECRET ABOUT CELEBRITY COOKBOOKS: THEY ALWAYS LEAVE A LITTLE SOMETHING out. Whether it's a drop of Madagascar vanilla, a squeeze of fresh lime, or a dash of fish sauce, the secret ingredient stays secret. Not that the recipes aren't terrific, but they're not the full story of what happens in the pro's kitchen.

I'm clearly not a celebrated chef (yet), but this is, in a certain sense, a book of recipes, recipes for collaboration, trust, and generosity. So it just wouldn't feel right to hold back the secret to what sets these activities apart and makes them so useful. I'm going to start off by handing over my chilled butter, my sprinkle of cinnamon, my secret ingredient: It's a tension I call "safe danger."

SAFETY

The psychologist Abraham Maslow mapped out a pyramid of what he called a person's hierarchy of needs. At the base of Maslow's pyramid are the most crucial things a person needs to survive from one day to the next: food, water, warmth, rest. Safety. With those in place you can move up the pyramid to relationships, belonging, self-esteem, and self-actualization. You need to be safe before you get to art, love, and enlightenment.

I'm sure there were early humans who valued art over safety. And I'm sure they were eaten by sabertooth tigers. We are descended from creatures of habit—and that habit is safety.

The early humans who found a reliable routine and stuck with it got enough nutrition and lived long enough to reproduce, and so that's the trait that got passed down to us. It makes sense that so many of us are inclined to overindex on safety—not just physical safety but also psychological and emotional safety as well. The cruelly ironic twist, of course, is that one of the best ways to fuel art, love, and enlightenment is to risk the safety that makes them possible.

DANGER

Danger is one of the best catalysts for meaningful growth. We know this instinctively. Ancient rites of passage were steeped in peril. Now, we seek it out for special occasions such as skydiving on a big birthday. Or as a forcing function, such as ropes courses for troubled teens, who, dangling thirty feet in the air, hearts pounding, learn to trust each other, learn their limits, and discover how to move beyond them. Because they have to. Because gravity. Because or else.

Growth and danger go hand in hand. You can't learn to walk without risking falling. You can't learn to love without risking heartbreak. There's no growth without risk, because growth means leaving the familiar behind, and that's always a risk.

This is not to suggest that we should be wildly reckless with ourselves in the name of growth, just that it's quite easy for safety to atrophy into stagnation. Once, when I was at a crossroads of life choices, I had a wild dream in which a *(clears throat)* neon turtle told me, "You can be safe, or you can dance." As a deep introvert, that's a horrifying choice. But even the turtle must emerge from its shell if it wants to move forward.[1] #turtlewisdom.

SAFE + DANGER = IMPACT

There are times to fracture the self, shake people up, rattle them—boot camp, therapy, ayahuasca, Christopher Nolan films. My activities are not that. Mine are gentler moments of disruption.

When I first began designing the safe danger activities to fuel the IDEO culture, I wanted a gentle way to build emotional muscle memory. Just like you don't only run the day of the marathon, I wanted a way to practice those qualities, build those muscles, with a manageable amount of discomfort. Muscles are built by tearing—the strain of exercise pulls your tiny muscle fibers apart so that they can knit themselves back together a little bit stronger than before. But it's a delicate balance—you don't want to shred them so drastically that you end up hobbling through the next few weeks in pain. No, you want to build muscle day by day, little by little over time. I wanted activities that would stress those emotional muscles, that sense of self and safety, enough to start to tear them, but only in the name of growing stronger. That way (1) growth wouldn't have to wait for some major marathon day, and (2) when that major day did come, we'd be in shape to really make the most of it. We'd have learned the tips and tricks, mapped our strengths and weaknesses, and completed preparations to get the most from the moment.

When I was first thinking through these activities, I had two goals: reassure and surprise. In that order. First, I wanted to reassure people that they were safe enough to loosen their grip on the familiar. Then I wanted them to find something unexpected that they would want to reach out and embrace with that newly opened hand. By adding a little danger, I was able to create the kind of safety that helps people feel sparked instead of stifled. By weaving in a little safety, I could deliver a kind of danger that helps people feel thrilled instead of threatened. And so I hit on this paradoxical balance of opposing currents: safe danger. Risk, yes, but without serious consequences. Vulnerable, yes, but without feeling exposed. Seen, yes, but without feeling judged.

So many forms of entertainment do little more than pass the time. From infinite scrolls to trivia nights, when you look back the only thing that moved forward were the hands of the clock. Safe danger is what makes the activities in this book different. Because, if people are comfortable enough to take a risk, they can really get something meaningful out of the time together and end the activity as a slightly different version of the person they were at the start—a little more connected, a little more insightful, a little more inspired. Safe danger is the secret ingredient that moves an activity from "pass the time" to "worth the time."

EVERYONE HATES TEAM BUILDING

Okay, well, maybe not everyone, but generally speaking, most people roll their eyes or, at best, are mostly just grateful for any break from work. Everyone has their own reasons for it—it takes time away from urgent projects, it feels forced, it feels uncomfortable, it feels artificial, it feels unproductive, it feels childish, it goes nowhere and has no lasting impact. As I've mentioned before, I agree. I hate team building. I didn't want to build a balloon tower that we'd never think about again or prove my value through trivia. Other people have their own hangups about it, which have come pouring out across the internet in threads like, "Team building is a useless waste of money. Prove me wrong," or "Keep your team building and just let me go home early to my family."

Regardless of the specific gripe, I get it. That's why my absolute favorite thing is when, after a session, someone makes their way over to me and announces, "I have to tell you, I was absolutely dreading this and almost skipped it. But this was amazing." The first time I heard that, I suspected we were on to something. By the hundredth, I was sure of it. It's not team building that is failing people; it's the types of team building we're used to.

I'm going to talk a lot about team building even though I realize not everyone works on a formal team. However, most people work with other people or live with other people. And the ways that people try to connect across all those arenas can be improved with a little safe danger. Whether it's your office or your book club, team building should be about everyone finding and sharing their own unique voice. In fact, after years of working with a broad spectrum of big and tiny companies, entrepreneurs, clubs, nonprofits, and governments, it's crystal clear that despite most people's perception, the connection that comes from effective team building is not a nice-to-have; it's a need-to-have.

With that in mind, I'm going to share what I've learned about why it's important, what gets in the way, and how to do it better. (Spoiler: It involves safe danger.)

WHY TEAM BUILDING IS SO IMPORTANT

Let's start with Elmo. Did you know that Elmo has his own social media account? Of course he does. My cat's chew toy has one. Elmo uses his to wish people a nice day, tell silly jokes, and model what being a friend can look like. At the beginning of 2024, Elmo posted a question to his friends: "How is everybody doing?" By the end of that first day, he had a whopping twenty thousand responses. But they weren't the sort of responses Elmo was expecting.

"Truly a roller-coaster ride of disappointment and self-doubt. Been on this planet nearly sixty-one years and feel I have no purpose anymore. It's all pointless. Cannot see where I fit anymore."

"It's been a tough time since we left Sesame Street and entered the workforce, Elmo."

"My job is a joke, Elmo. But without the laughter."

"Every morning, I cannot wait to go back to sleep. Every Monday, I cannot wait for Friday to come. Every single day and every single week for life."

I suspect Elmo started rethinking his decision to apply for that summer internship.

Of the thousands and thousands of responses, the two dominant themes were climate change and work life. In the collective psyche, job dissatisfaction is on equal footing with the death of the planet.

And Elmo is not the only one who has noticed the state of the working world.

For years Dr. Vivek Murthy, former surgeon general of the United States, has been using his platform to talk about what he calls the loneliness epidemic.

He means it when he calls it an epidemic. Fifty percent of Americans report experiencing loneliness on a regular basis.[2] It turns out loneliness is pretty awful for your mental, emotional, and physical health. It's tied to heart disease, dementia, stroke, depression, anxiety, and that charming catch-all, premature death.

He points a finger squarely at our work culture as a critical problem area. "People sit in an office full of coworkers but everyone is staring at a computer or in meetings where opportunities to connect on a human level are scarce."[3]

It seems like much of the working world is feeling disconnected and disengaged. There's been the great resignation, quiet quitting, and quick quitting; the fact that we're constantly having to invent clever new names for all the ways we're disappointed with our work life is telling in and of itself. But year after year Gallup's *State of the Global Workplace* report makes it crystal clear that the old methods of retaining talent are not resonating in the workplace today.

From the mailroom to the C-suite, over half of today's employees are looking to find something new, particularly a place that cares more about their well-being.[4]

"At least he died doing what he loved."

Even the people who aren't looking for a new job aren't doing a very good job. The majority of the world's employees, 70 percent, are quiet quitting—they don't really know how to do their jobs or why their work matters, and they don't have any real bonds with their coworkers, boss, or the organization itself.[5] They don't care. They don't feel cared about.

But they want that to change. Employees were asked, "If you could make *one* change at your current employer to make it a great place to work, what would it be?" It's no surprise that 28 percent said *better pay and better benefits* because most of us go to work to make money. What is surprising is that almost double said *the most important factor* was engagement, culture, or well-being.[6]

They want to feel cared about. They want to feel connected. And this echoes a sentiment I've heard from many chief people officers and talent managers: People come to work for the paycheck, but they stay where they work for the people.

It's not just the quiet quitters who feel this way. Eighty-two percent of all the employees surveyed say it's important that their organizations see them as a whole person. And management knows this makes a difference: 92 percent of executives agree that high employee engagement leads to happier customers.[7]

The takeaway, from Elmo and the surgeon general to the quiet quitters, is that connection is crucial for both your mental and your physical well-being.

Now, I've been to plenty of conferences and heard plenty of people talking about how important authentic connection is in the workplace. However, I've found that when push comes to shove and it's time to allocate the two things that really show where your true values lie—time and money—*connection* shifts right back into the nice-to-have category and is the first to get cut.

So, in case you ever need to convince someone that better connection is worth the investment, I want to share some real-world business facts that stand apart from the feelings.

First of all, better connection means better employees.

When companies with low to average employee engagement are compared to companies with high scores for connection and engagement, the advantages come spilling out. Employees who felt connected and engaged delivered more work (21 percent increase in productivity), delivered better-quality work (41 percent fewer product defects), were happier and healthier doing so (17 percent better physical health, 23 percent better mental health), were almost 90 percent more loyal to their employers, and were 250 percent more likely to push themselves above and beyond to exceed performance expectations.[8]

Better connection also means better business overall. Companies with happy, engaged workforces outperform their competitors in earnings per share by almost 150 percent, according to Gallup's research. They make more (18 percent more sales, 23 percent more profitable), lose less time and fewer resources (28 percent less internal theft, 81 percent less absenteeism), and are better at retaining both customers and talent (28 percent higher customer loyalty, 81 percent lower turnover).[9]

If better connection means better employees, better teams, and better business, what gets in the way?

WHAT GETS IN THE WAY

When groups want to build an engaged and connected culture, they turn to team-building activities. There are plenty of options out there, from scavenger hunts to cooking classes. In my time, I've done everything from axe throwing to flower arranging, and I'm sure you've done many of them as well. There's a whole spectrum of options, but what all these team-building activities have in common is that they're fun. It's lovely to go for a boat cruise. It's exciting to win at trivia. It's fun to escape from a room. So, what more do you need? With a spread from mini golf to murder mysteries, what could be missing?

Team building is usually about a shared experience. Whether it's a contest or a class, as long as you're doing something fun together, that generally counts as team building. And yes, fun, nonwork, shared experiences are a critical ingredient for connection. But what most people don't realize is that it takes more than that one ingredient. Connection takes more than just sharing the same space or experience, no matter how fun that experience may be in the moment. In fact, sometimes the nature of a shared experience can actually interfere with building a lasting, quality connection. In my experience and from feedback from clients, three qualities in common team-building efforts derail lasting positive impact on a team's long-term behavior: competition, passivity, and old news.

Competition: By its very nature competition divides people and pits them against each other. Not a great mindset if you're after trust and understanding. Also, most people lose. That rarely feels good, but even winning is counterproductive. Competition celebrates what you do instead of who you are. People are proud of their accomplishments, love winning games, enjoy looking good, and all the rest. But, ultimately, we still want to know we'll be loved even if we lose, get saggy, and stumble. At our core, most of us want to be valued without having to prove our value.

Passivity: Passive activities are the ones where you're basically an entertained audience member. It doesn't matter if you're engaged, paying attention, or even there at all. Participants don't contribute anything of themselves to the experience.

Old News: By *old news*, I mean that the traits you already see in the workplace just get bigger. The loud get louder. The quiet get quieter. The cliques huddle together. You don't learn anything new about each other.

When people say they hate team building, it's usually because they don't like competition, they're bored in the audience, or they'd rather be doing things or spending time with people they really care about. Essentially, regular team building feels uncomfortable and like a waste of time. As fun as passive entertainment and active competition can be, they can derail opportunities to connect in the most impactful and lasting ways.

So, how do you design, think through, or select activities that are going to reach people? What makes the difference? Okay. Here is the least professional line in this whole book, but I'm going to share it anyway and hope that you can stomach it:

Everyone wants to feel loved.

Record scratch moment, I know. But stay with me. I reluctantly backed into this conclusion because of the feedback I got from people who repeatedly came to my activities—what they came back for, what they missed when I left it out, how they described the activities to others. And when I looked at the common thread, it was that they felt seen and important, but not judged. They were able to be vulnerable without feeling threatened. They felt they had value to offer that was appreciated. In essence, it was the feeling of being loved.

From a ten-thousand-foot view, you can look at this through an anthropological lens: As social animals, we're hardwired to want to be valued by our peers, the same way we're wired to find water beautiful and the colors of ripe fruit appetizing. Nutrition, procreation, shelter, survival have all depended on it since the Pleistocene. Feeling loved is one of our most primal, fundamental needs.

You're wanted, you're welcomed, you're important, and you're safe.

What's better than that? Not much.

What does that have to do with team building? Not much.

Usually.

But if you look at the dynamics of what motivates people, what builds loyalty, what encourages connection, it's immensely helpful to go to the source and then work back from there to an appropriate level. That's why, yes, I am absolutely talking about feeling loved. But, no, I am absolutely not saying that the workplace or your neighborhood should be a kumbaya festival of flower crowns and Hallmark cards. That would not be an appropriate level. Do not go around offering free hugs. *Do* think about why people in every culture enjoy wrapping their arms around each other in times of joy and sadness. That's where the insight can bubble up.

When I design activities, I avoid competition because it has only a certain amount of love to go around; I avoid activities that are passive because they don't single people out enough to feel loved; and I avoid activities that just amplify because they don't create opportunities to discover new things to love in others.

HOW TO DO IT BETTER

Okay, so let's talk about a different approach to team building. If I'm not thrilled with competition, passivity, and amplification, what do I look for when designing an activity?

In place of competition, which puts everyone's defenses up, I use safe danger to lower those defenses and make it easier for people to get vulnerable and open up to each other. Instead of something they just absorb, I use safe danger to make it easy for everyone to add something of themselves to the experience. Finally, instead of amplifying familiar behaviors, I use safe danger to help colleagues better understand those behaviors.

From	→	**To**
Competition	→	Connection
Passivity	→	Participation
Old News	→	New Insight

CONNECTION

As the surgeon general put it so well, "We spend more waking hours with our co-workers than we do with our families. But do they know what we really care about? Do they understand our values? Do they share in our triumphs and pains?"[10] I use this mash-up of safe danger to broaden, deepen, and accelerate meaningful connection, to help colleagues learn what you really care about, really understand your values, and genuinely share in your triumphs and pains. As fun as it may be, that sort of insight just doesn't *usually* come from beating someone at mini golf.

PARTICIPATION

People love free things, but they don't value them. The social scientist Dan Ariely calls this the "Ikea effect," and his research has shown that people place a higher value on items they have invested effort or money into, even if that investment is tiny. The act of contributing something of oneself creates a sense of ownership and investment, leading people to ascribe greater value to the item, regardless of its actual worth. A fun example of this is the egg you add to boxed cake mix. There's no reason the mix couldn't already include that egg. In fact, it originally did. But sales were dismal. Then they took the egg out and asked you to add it. Sales skyrocketed. That egg was enough for people to feel a sense of ownership and investment in the cake so that they could produce something they felt they had made.

That's why I design activities so that participants have to contribute something of themselves. It's not a free ride—the activity doesn't work unless they pick up an oar and help row. That way they have some skin in the game, and they know it matters that they are there. Everyone both gives and receives, learns and teaches, bows and applauds. The trick here is to make it so seamless and fun that no one feels forced, and everyone gets the benefits without noticing the cost.

NEW INSIGHT

Why is Pat such a people pleaser? *Why* is it so important for Charles to be in charge? I look for ways to design activities so that people walk away with a better understanding of themselves and their colleagues. More empathy for others and more patience for themselves. One key thing professional mediators look for when helping to resolve conflict is common ground. What shared traits, beliefs, goals, fears, and so forth do people have in common that can be used to build a stronger, more productive connection? I try to help people identify and articulate what drives their behaviors so that people who may have very different backgrounds, profiles, personalities, or behaviors can still find a bridge with which to easily build productive bonds.

People may still prefer spending time on passion projects or with family to team building, but if done right, team building not only has an impact on the work culture but also benefits those passion projects and family relations as well.

Okay. That's a lovely sentiment, but how do you work such witchcraft?

That's where safe danger comes in.

As the rest of this section describes, most of my activities are designed to nudge people out of their professional comfort zones. Depending on the activity, I may be asking them to risk looking unprofessional, risk making mistakes, risk sharing personal stories, and, frankly, risk rethinking the way their day-to-day typically runs. That's a lot to ask of someone, especially in the non sequitur context of a team-building event that typically happens sandwiched in a workday when most people are trying to live up to their résumés or at an offsite with people they've just met.

If I'm going to invite people into that dangerously unprofessional territory, I need to make sure to design the activity with guardrails that let a wide variety of people feel safe to be themselves, safe to admit their mistakes and learn from them, safe to contribute from personal experience, and safe to speak out about how they'd like things to change.

Essentially, I want to reassure people that they're safe enough to release their grip on the way things are normally done. Then, I can take that open hand and lead them somewhere new. I can show them that the dangerous territory they normally keep guarded isn't really that dangerous.

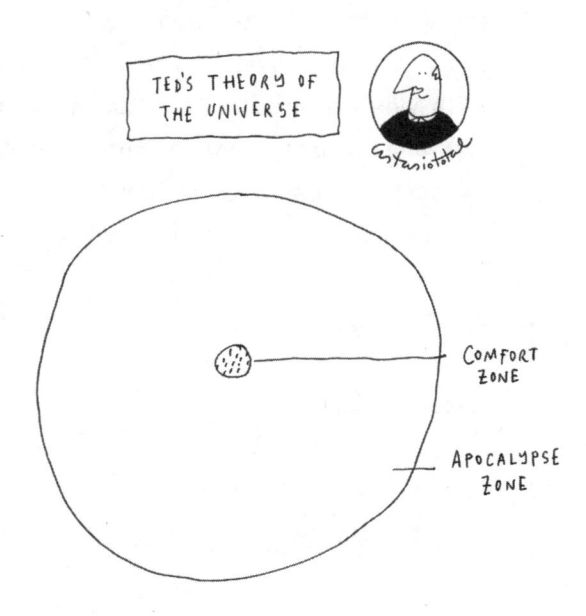

This is obviously a delicate balancing act. Figuring out a way to help people rapidly lower their guard and start trusting each other is a tall order. But it's essential if you want people to understand each other. That's why I want to make sure that, just like all the other team-building activities, this time spent together should feel fun and joyful. So I use art and play to make it possible. This is where the oven mitts of creativity come into play and give us a safe way to handle this dangerous material.

ACTIVITY

Super Secret

When Galactic Guardian met Flexy Fox for the first time, she asked if Flexy Fox's puppy was feeling better. Flexy Fox wanted to know about Galactic Guardian's recent birthday. There were no awkward silences, even though Galactic Guardian and Flexy Fox were, until this very moment, complete strangers.

Well, not complete strangers. They had shared an unusual experience over the previous five weeks, an activity called Super Secret.

In the spring of 2020, as the pandemic was first flexing its muscles and shutting down the world, a select group of forty people received bright yellow packages. Quantum Questioner tore his open with his teeth, whereas Disco Diva used an heirloom antique letter opener, but everyone found the same contents inside. Five prestamped bright yellow postcards with weekly prompts. Materials for drawing on or decorating the postcards. And an invitation:

We are facing an honest-to-goodness villain set on world domination.
Our way of life is under threat.
Innocent people are isolated and alone, cut off from each other.
This is the time for the heroes to put on their capes.
This is the moment that's been waiting for you.
It's time to be super.

*If you can fly, grow laser claws, write a story, draw a picture,
or even just turn invisible, we need you.
Your supersecret mission: reach out across the isolation to one
other person. Let them know who you are. Listen to who they are.
Let them know that someone super is thinking about them.*

*The task is crucial; the ask is simple:
Get to know your partner.
You've been given five prompts, one per week, that will ask you to share a secret piece of your story with both words and pictures—you will write your story on one side and create a visual on the other side, then mail it off to your partner. They will be doing the same (unless they are being stomped on by a T. rex).*

*Don't worry, they're pretty light secrets. No PIN codes or passwords.
They're "secrets" in the sense that they're not the sort of thing just anyone will know about you.
You can share your preferred superhero name,
but please do not reveal your secret identity.
No names. No hair color. No descriptions.
Just stories.
(Please note: Boring answers will be disintegrated by laser sharks.)*

*You and your partners are each going to start off as anonymous mysteries to the other.
But this isn't about solving that mystery. It's not about finding clues to figure out who they are.
It's the opposite. Embrace the anonymity.
Be generous with what you share.
Be thoughtful about how you respond.
Be kind.
(Watch the mail with eagle eyes and catlike reflexes for your partner's answers to arrive.)*

After five weeks of sharing stories through the mail, you will take what you've learned about your partner, their powers, their kryptonite, and use it to create a final product....
...but that's all we can tell you right now.
After all, this is supersecret!

The prompts started with fun, happy secrets. Super Swifty answered No. 1—Share the Secret of Your Stuffed Animal—by talking about Platypurp the Purple Platypus.

For one of the most embarrassing memories requested by prompt No. 3, Hoppy Hippopotomonstrosesquippedaliophobia shared the story of his thirteen-year-old self's first kiss. It was with a girl he'd been pining after for years, in a dark closet during a birthday party round of "Seven Minutes in Heaven." After about the third minute, with his pulse pounding in his ears and his lungs working overtime, she'd pulled her lips away from his and said, in a kind voice, "You don't do this very often, do you?" The kindness that still stung.

By the time the heroes reached No. 5 ("What three qualities do you and your partner have in common?") Furious Flappybrain had plenty to work with. From the Neatness Ninja's answers, she knew they both hated disappointing others, both felt refueled by nature, and both loved chocolate milk.

After the last secrets were exchanged, a date was set for a big reveal Zoom party, and each partner was invited to make and send a gift to the other: a superhero mask that reflected all they had learned about each other using the pom-poms, pipe cleaners, mirrors, gems, stickers, and beads they'd received five weeks earlier in that big yellow package. Everyone showed up on-screen wearing their gifted masks—although they had been exchanging stories for weeks, this was the first time they were seeing each other. They exploded in laughter.

Half the partners were eight years old and the other half closer to eighty.

We had paired a class of fourth graders whose school had shut down with the residents of a senior home who were on a social-distancing lockdown. Some had suspected. Although they all started out assuming they were corresponding with peers, some fourth graders caught on when their partner recounted "A Cherished Memory" as the day they became a grandparent, and some seniors were tipped off by an enthusiasm for Taylor Swift uncommon among the Greatest Generation. Regardless, conversations between partners went twice as long as planned and there was a general request from both sides (yes, even the kids) for permission to continue the correspondence on their own.

I have since adapted and deployed the Super Secret activity to work virtually and in-person as well as through the mail. I've used it with groups of hundreds of strangers, I've used it with small teams who have worked together for years. I've used it with companies looking to activate diversity, equity, and inclusion (DEI) learning in an experiential way. I've seen it bridge divergent points of view related to politics, race, economics, gender, geography, and religion. Although there are naturally different takeaways and goals for the different groups, what is consistent is the surprise and satisfaction on people's faces after they've connected in a meaningful way.

According to the people who study joy and happiness for a living, a key factor that determines our personal and professional happiness is meaningful connection with other people. However, as we all know, being with other people is not the same as being connected with them. Not in a meaningful way.

Yet, what this activity asks of people, to drop their guard a bit, to let someone else see some of the secret parts of their life, and—maybe more importantly—to let someone else share with them, that's the dynamic that really makes the difference. People feel like they matter to each other. That fuels meaningful connection.

But that's a lot to ask of strangers out of nowhere. It would be a lot of danger to dump on them all at once. So, we temper the danger by stirring a little safety into the mix.

Three important elements in Super Secret help facilitate and regulate the interplay of safety and danger:

1. **Anonymity:** The less we know about someone, the easier it is to dress them up and see them exactly as we wish. It helps quiet any biases and it makes the activity about character, not characteristics.
2. **Story:** To build connection and not just exchange information, we swapped small talk for questions that reveal something more personal.
3. **Play:** Play is the part that's most often overlooked, but it's the glue that holds it all together. It lightens the mood, relaxes the defenses, and lets you just be you without worrying about impressing other people.

SUPER SECRET: CHARACTER, NOT CHARACTERISTICS

Primary Quality
Connection

Supporting Themes
Trust
Empathy
Questioning Assumptions

The What

Connecting across distance and difference. A simple yet powerful digital twist on the pen pal dynamic that builds connection based on meaning, not appearance.

The How

Pair Up: Participants turn off their cameras, mics, and change their screen names to a made-up superhero name that reflects their character. They are paired up anonymously—no names, no images, no voices—and put into breakout rooms.

Connect: The facilitator shares five prompts, one every five minutes, for the partners to discuss through the chat.

1. The secret of the stuffed animal you had as a child
2. The secret of one of your most cherished memories
3. The secret of a challenge you overcame
4. The secret of one of your most embarrassing moments
5. Three qualities we have in common

Create: Each participant then takes five minutes to create a drawing of the other as a superhero, complete with powers and characteristics based on the stories they've exchanged.

Reveal: The partners turn their screens on and exchange the gifts they've made for each other. Then everyone returns to the main room for an open floor. Close with the why.

The Why

One of the key hallmarks of this moment in history is how we perceive difference. This is an incredibly fraught question, with two main currents running through it: a desire to focus on what we have in common, and a desire to focus on what makes us unique. And though these two are not inherently mutually exclusive, anger, fear, ignorance, and frustration often reduce them to enemies. We see this play out every day. One positive interaction is not going to solve that. But sharing personal stories opens an opportunity to celebrate both of those strains simultaneously and use that as a way to connect more deeply with each other.

Personal stories let us make our introductions from the inside out.

Super Secret cultivates a culture of empathy and compassion by building meaningful bridges between people who may otherwise appear very different. The prompts are crafted to spotlight values and feelings so that the anonymous pair develop a relationship built on character rather than characteristics.

The careful combination of anonymity, story, and play helps people hear their partner and themselves in a new way. The freedom of anonymity encourages honesty because participants don't know who to tailor their responses for, the playful dynamic lowers the bar for engagement, and the personal stories allow finding common ground in shared feelings.

Participants walk away with a little more practice in the emotional skills we all need to see the world through a more diverse lens. In a professional setting, this can lead to the sort of trust, collaboration, and creative confidence that makes for strong, innovative teams.

The Materials

Video conference software with the capability to broadcast into breakout rooms

WHY PLAY AT WORK?

Despite the reluctance to welcome play in most professional settings on a regular basis, a seemingly endless river of research shows how beneficial play is for work: Employees who have access to playful activities at work report a 12 percent increase in *productivity*;[11] workplaces that encourage playfulness see a 20 percent boost in employee *creativity and innovation*;[12] and employees in playful work environments report a 15 percent higher *job satisfaction* rate compared to those in more serious settings.[13] Incorporating play into the workday is proven to significantly reduce employee *stress levels*;[14] teams that engage in regular playful activities show up to 30 percent improvement in *collaboration* and teamwork;[15] playful work environments are associated with a 40 percent reduction in employee *absenteeism*;[16] companies that promote playfulness experience a 17 percent increase in *employee engagement*;[17] employees who engage in playful thinking are 30 percent better at *problem-solving* and generating new ideas;[18] and companies known for their playful and innovative cultures attract 25 percent more *high-quality job candidates*.[19] And on and on and on.

As I said, the goal of my activities is better connection and more understanding at work, so I use play as a way to lower the stakes and raise the joy. But the research shows that a playful connection activity is a twofer because bringing play to the work culture also has powerful benefits in its own right.

WHY PLAY AT HOME?

But maybe your workplace culture just isn't ready to welcome an element of play. Maybe it's too much of a stretch for them to believe that being unproductive can make you more productive. That doesn't mean you should forfeit your own interest in play. Study after study shows that a person's play experiences have a profound influence on the shape and quality of their lives: "Very accomplished people tend to have lives that allow and embrace play, and those with unhealthy, rigid, unproductive behaviors are often seriously play deprived."[20]

Obviously, my strong preference is to bring joy and play into the workplace, but that doesn't mean you have to leave your ability to play in the hands of your job. The fact is, for those willing to make the time, the emotional, mental, and physical benefits of play are just waiting for you to reach out and claim them:

- *Better Relationships:* Couples who engage in playful activities together report a 30 percent increase in relationship satisfaction and emotional intimacy.[21]
- *Better Connections:* Engaging in playful activities with others increases social bonds and reduces feelings of loneliness.[22]
- *Better Brains:* Seniors who regularly engage in playful activities show a 20 percent slower decline in cognitive functions, such as memory and attention.[23]

- *Better Stress Management:* Regular play can reduce levels of cortisol, the stress hormone, by up to 30 percent.[24]
- *Better Mental Health:* Adults who engage in regular playful activities experience a significant reduction in symptoms of depression.[25]
- *Better Thinking:* Adults who maintain playful hobbies outside of work are 35 percent more likely to exhibit creative thinking and problem-solving skills in their professional lives.[26]
- *Better Life:* Playful adults have been shown to have significantly greater life satisfaction and emotional well-being.[27]

In this book, I'm of course pushing for team building at work. But the good news is that you don't need to be an employee at a company to benefit and use these exercises. I've done these activities with groups of friends, I've done them with my family, and I've even done activities solo (more on that later). The heart of safe danger is deceptively simple: Make people feel safe and then use that trust to nudge them out of their comfort zone. It's a simple but powerful approach that anyone can use to deepen their connections and broaden their thinking.

HABIT BUILDER

Honest Answers

Getting vulnerable can often be intimidating because it feels like an all-or-nothing proposition. Either you open the door wide to the world or you lock it tight. But even if that's how it feels, that is not the truth. You can risk opening up a little at a time.

What would happen if, for a week, you tried to answer honestly when people ask how you're doing? Instead of "Fine.

How are you doing?" You could say, "I'm trying to shake off my commute," or "I'm smiling on the inside because of this silly dream I had."

This isn't an invitation to list off all the medications you're taking or unload like the conference table is a therapist's couch. Just give them a sense of what's making your day different from theirs. What you're carrying beneath the "I've got it all together" attitude. Maybe people will nod, maybe they'll empathize. Maybe not. It doesn't matter, because you've opened the door a little and risked sharing a little of yourself.

CHAPTER TWO

SAFETY THAT SPARKS INSTEAD OF STAGNATES

"THIS IS A SAFE SPACE."

No, it's not. Not if you have to tell me it is.

My eleven-year-old came home from school one day overflowing with questions and opinions about a particularly controversial topic they'd discussed in her humanities class. I asked how the class had responded to her ideas. "Oh, I didn't say any of that out loud. Nobody ever says anything different than what the teacher says. She always says it's a safe space to share our thoughts and ask questions, but kids don't stop judging you just because she tells them not to."

Just like "We love our customers," "That's funny," or, "I'm not angry," if it was true, you wouldn't need to say, "This is a safe space." I've heard that phrase uttered in office gatherings many, many times by very well-meaning people. During social upheavals. In the midst of elections. After verdicts. It never means anything. If it wasn't a safe space before those words were spoken, the declaration isn't going to change a thing. Because safety isn't about the space or the moment. It's about the people and their relationships to each other. Psychological safety isn't announced; it's earned.

This chapter is all about the type of safety that's worth earning.

"Go on, Knuckles, this is a safe space."

GOOGLE IT

Google wants its teams to be the best of the best. So the company invested two years of its time and money into researching how to optimize team performance and get the most out of its people. When a place with the resources of Google does a deep dive into success, the results are definitely worth a listen.[1] What Google found is that its highest-performing teams have one thing in common. Not talent. Not education. Not shared purpose. Not work styles. Not salary levels. Not even personality typology. What the highest-performing teams have in common is psychological safety.

Psychological safety means that you feel:

Safe to Be Yourself: Everyone can share thoughts, emotions, and their authentic self without repercussions or fear of judgment.

Safe to Learn: Everyone is encouraged to explore new ideas, ask questions, and admit mistakes.

Safe to Contribute: Everyone's input is welcomed and respected regardless of rank or status.

Safe to Challenge: Dissenting opinions or alternative solutions don't invite negative consequences or retaliation.

Are you comfortable doing all four of these? Are the people you're responsible for? What Google discovered is that what really makes the difference is not *who* is working together on the team, but *how* the team works together. Teams with high psychological safety have lower turnover, are better at capitalizing on their ideas, are more productive, are more profitable, and are more loyal to their organization as a whole.[2] The highest-performing teams feel safe to be themselves, safe to acknowledge and learn from mistakes, safe to add their voice, and safe to question others. That's not an easy dynamic to achieve in a world of tight deadlines, competitive markets, career ambitions, and shareholder reports. It's not an easy dynamic to achieve in a family where everyone has different priorities, interests, and sensitivities. But in both cases the effort seems to pay off.

This isn't just about how people consciously choose to treat others. Lack of psychological safety may literally impair our ability to think. Disapproval from a boss, competition from a coworker, or ridicule from a peer throws our brain into crisis mode, and on a physiological level we react to it as a life-or-death threat. The amygdala sets off mental alarm bells, fires up the ol' fight-or-flight instinct, hijacks the higher brain centers, shuts down perspective and analytic reasoning, and kneecaps our strategic thinking abilities right when we need them most.

This is not your fault. If you have a brain, this is how it works. You can't change that. What can be changed is the emotional environment so that questions aren't seen as attacks and mistakes aren't felt as weakness.[3] Research shows that positive emotions such as trust, curiosity, confidence, and inspiration make your brain feel safe and emotionally secure, and that makes you a better problem solver, a more nuanced critical thinker, a more open-minded, resilient, motivated, persistent, and funny person.

TEAM EFFORT

Creating and maintaining psychological safety isn't easy or fast. It requires attention and intention from everyone involved, whether that means spouses, parents and children, or established leaders and new hires. It's like a choir. Once you get everyone on the same page, singing their parts in harmony, you can create something that's more than the sum of its parts. At the same time, it doesn't take many sour notes to disrupt that harmony. That's why it's important to think of this as a practice rather than as a one-and-done.

To gauge people's emotional states, some well-meaning companies do "pulse checks" and some self-aware couples schedule "relationship check-ins" to determine whether others are feeling enough psychological safety. Though I respect the effort, my suggestion is to just assume they're not. Use those pulse checks and check-ins to find out how to do better. How can you make people feel respected and cared for? Show, don't tell. Words like "You're important to me" should feel as unnecessary as instructions on soap.

Many experts advise leaders to establish psychological safety by modeling the vulnerability they hope to encourage. They suggest that if leaders want their team to feel comfortable taking risks, they should be transparent about their own mistakes to demonstrate that no one is expected to be perfect. I'm all for this. It's made a huge difference for me when my leaders have shown up this way. But many leaders fear that if they're not seen as having it all together at all times, their people will lose confidence. Truth be told, they have a point.

So, what's the secret? Context. Successful vulnerability is a two-way street. It's not just about rolling over and showing your belly. Yes, someone needs to be brave enough to go first, but you need to prep your audience to receive that vulnerability as intended. That's one of the reasons I like using controlled moments of play and creativity for moving into this territory—leaders can model vulnerability, but in this context their teams also reciprocate immediately so that they get a feel for the language of authenticity. I think of it like teaching a young kid to play catch. They can't just practice catching. They need to know what it feels like to throw so that they can calibrate their own efforts, knowing full well what it feels like to be on both sides of the ball.

HELP WANTED

How you feel about asking for help is an excellent barometer of psychological safety. I mentioned this earlier, but it's worth returning to. Most of the places I've worked have encouraged people to ask for help if they need it. But they didn't really mean it. In subtle and not-so-subtle ways, their cultures made it clear that needing help was a sign of incompetence, an imposition on others, and ultimately the sign of a follower rather than a leader.

Then I went to IDEO. In its culture, asking for help was seen as the biggest compliment you could bestow on a peer. It showed respect, humility, and a desire to deliver the best results possible. Inevitably, we all knew that helping others helped us hone our own skills, exposed us to new thinking and problems, and elevated the work we were proud of adding to the world.[4]

SAFETY IN ACTION

You don't need to use play to bolster those four elements of psychological safety. Especially not in the workplace, where it's not always welcome. But it's much more effective to build an environment of safety through experiences than by announcing it through a handout or policy. Psychological safety is not a fact unless it's felt.

ACTIVITY

Moving Stories

By far one of my most uncomfortable activities is called Moving Stories. Historically, this is the one that gives people the most pause because part of the activity involves—I hesitate to admit—interpretive dance. There's really no middle ground with interpretive dance. You either live for it or would rather die. Most people are on the latter side. Myself included. Yet it's absolutely one of the most useful activities in my library.

The premise is simple. I ask everyone to think about their inner experience of going from being blocked to being inspired. I ask them to draw out that experience as a squiggle. A swirling tornado of frustration? A panicked EKG? A meandering seagull's path? Everyone has their own process. And after they squiggle theirs out, I ask them to share their process with the rest of us. But not the squiggle they drew. I ask them to tell that story with their body. With motion. With a dance.

People love taking personality tests. I'm a 5w4 on the Enneagram. INTP according to Myers-Briggs. I rate highest on Explore on the 5 Dynamics energy test. I like to generate together and refine alone. Yadda yadda. I've discovered all these things during HR retreats and team kick-off meetings. It's meant to help us understand each other and ourselves better. I'm also a Ravenclaw, a John Lennon, a Jim Halpert, a Samantha, a Grover, a Chaotic Neutral, and a Capybara, according to a battery of other personality tests.

Personality tests are fun and easy, and people love hearing about themselves. The problem is that the insights are delivered to the analytical mind. Intellectually, people may learn some things about themselves, but behavior tends to be determined on a more intuitive and less rational level. The tests may ask about your feelings, but there's no feeling involved. The results may give you a target to aim for and adjust, but they don't give you the emotional muscle memory to go after it. Nothing ventured, nothing earned.

The value of the Moving Stories activity is that it's a personality test both taken and shared through an intuitive experience. The *content* of the activity isn't asking people to stick their necks out by sharing anything startling. But the *method* is. Making people tell their stories without words brings instinct and intuition into the mix, which opens room for new insights that the analytic mind might gloss over. It delivers information to the audience in a new and memorable way that invites more dimensions of understanding. Most importantly, it immerses people in the qualities they're trying to reckon with. It lets them *feel* empathy, discomfort, trust, failure, and hope with their body. And that thirty minutes of active practice is more valuable than three hundred pages of test results.

But, as I said, most people would rather scrub grout than get their Martha Graham on. So, how to keep the benefits of the danger and still make it safe?

Make It Easy

As I mentioned, this is not an activity I would welcome personally. So, when I designed it, I took myself through it and tried to bubble-wrap as many of the jagged experiential corners as possible. For example, like many people who sing in the shower or in their car, I'm perfectly comfortable dancing at home. Alone. With the curtains pulled. Maybe with the lights off. So, I tried to address the embarrassment of being watched in the activity's design. To start with, I have everyone wear colorful sleep masks while they're choreographing their dance. This helps them block out the rest of the world and focus inward. Everyone is free to create in a private moment when they know they're not being watched or judged or being thought silly. Because, frankly, I want them to move in silly ways, to check their dignity at the door, and to share in a way that is honest and authentic.

I also make sure to distribute the discomfort. Instead of having them perform their dance for each other solo, I bundle them into small cohorts and have them teach their dance to the others who will be their backup dancers. This switches the power dynamic from being evaluated to being the evaluator. At some point everyone is the teacher and everyone is the student. No one is singled out. This also means that during the performance they're not the only ones on display, and they're being supported by their backup dancers, so it's a group effort.

Finally, there's the applause. At the end of every performance, we applaud. It's silly, but crucial. Everyone needs to feel equally appreciated.

Make It Okay

We don't usually express ourselves with our body so dramatically unless you live in a reenactment of *West Side Story* or *Step Up*. So, the first thing I do is acknowledge that. I'm clear that, of all my activities, this feels the least dignified, the least professional, the most vulnerable, and the most uncomfortable. I acknowledge that discomfort, but then I ask them to shake it off. If they're feeling nervous, I ask them to take off their anxiety, roll it into a ball, and put it over there in that corner for the next thirty minutes. I reassure them that it'll still be there when we're done if they want to retrieve it. But for the time being, I give them permission to just go with it so they don't have to take responsibility for looking silly. After all, they are just doing what I told them to do.

I show them it's okay by modeling it myself with a range of awkward dances and then I ask them to embrace the discomfort, laugh at themselves, laugh at each other with kindness and empathy, remember this is silly, this is out of the ordinary, and that's part of the fun.

And, finally, I give them an out... but an out that actually hides an invitation to go deeper in. I know for a lot of people this is too much, and if that's the case, I give them permission to step away and just watch. But I offer them this: "Part of the point of this activity is to make you a little uncomfortable. A little vulnerable. To practice putting yourself out there. This is your chance to cut loose and blame me. To be silly without judgment. How often are you invited to take a risk? So, if you opt to step away, I'd just ask you to consider under what circumstances you *would* be willing to take such a risk?"

Make It Valuable

After everyone has performed, I wrap up the experience by giving them a frame through which they can recount the experience when they retell it. Every time we retell a story, we reestablish our perspective on it. A neutral experience can be turned into a nightmare or a thrill ride over time depending on how we deliver the story to others.

I explain how this dance helps articulate things that we otherwise most likely would not think to share with each other and may not have even articulated to ourselves. I point out how it allows us to see each other's patterns. They now know that Njoki always goes forward and then takes a few steps backward and thinks it through again and again. So, if I'm working with her and I think we've solved it and suddenly she starts having second thoughts, I know it's not me. I know this is her process. And now I'm in a great position to either back off and let her work her way through it or work with her and help her move forward.

Now that they have seen and experienced each other's patterns, they can use those insights to improve their collaboration, refine their expectations, and target their support.

MOVING STORIES: THE UNSPOKEN MADE PHYSICAL

Primary Quality
Connection

Supporting Themes
Trust
Community
Storytelling

The What

Miming your mental process. People create a dance that articulates an internal process without using words, which asks them to slow down, reflect, and think about themselves through a new lens.

The How

Reflect: Everyone begins by reflecting on their experience of going from being frustrated by a challenge to being inspired with a solution. (A poet friend once suggested I simplify this to a typographical koan: ? → !) What is that process like on the inside? Using an empty sheet of paper, everyone begins by translating their process into a line squiggle that represents their journey from blocked to inspired. Is it a zigzag, an arch, a knot, a concentric spiral?

Then we move from two dimensions to three. Everyone dons a sleep mask so that no one can see anyone else, and everyone is secure in their own private moment. Then they translate their personal, emotional experience of going from frustration to inspiration into physical movement. Everyone creates a dance, using motion to tell their story.

Teach: When everyone is ready, the masks come off and the dance party begins. In groups of four, everyone takes turns teaching their dance to their three backup dancers, explaining the emotion behind each step, and rehearsing their group performance.

Perform: Each group performs the dances from all four members of their group. The audience applauds vigorously. Then the next group performs. Once everyone has performed, open the floor for comments, then close out with the why.

The Why

The shared nature of the activity helps everyone see into the experience of their teammates in a completely new way—both how they experience this process, and how they choose to convey it. Teaching our dance to others builds that vulnerability and trust that are so vital to real collaboration, because we go forward with the knowledge that somebody else knows us and we can trust them with that knowledge. Dancing someone else's dance ourselves can give us an inkling of what they feel and allows us to see, feel, and absorb each other's patterns.

This activity is a moment of vulnerability, of connection, and of understanding. A moment to learn about yourself as well as your friends, family, or colleagues. A moment of empathy beyond words.

The Materials

A rainbow of colored sleep masks

A SPRINKLING OF DANGER

If you want to spark change, you need to start by creating the conditions for it. You can have all the kerosene and matches you want, but if you're at the bottom of a pool, you're not getting that fire started. Similarly, you can bring in all the talent and software and materials you want, but if you're missing a culture that allows people to feel comfortable being themselves, learning, contributing, and challenging, then meaningful change is going to remain out of reach.

Some of my activities directly tackle psychological safety. Masking the Darkness (see page 235) is about revealing your full self. The heart of Unblinking Line (see page 126) is joyful failure, and Blobviously (see page 201) hinges

"Just have fun—and don't embarrass yourself, or me, or the team, or your parents, or your teachers, or your neighbors or..."

on unapologetically sharing your perspective. Orchestra of Optimism (see page 241) invites you to voice things that usually go unspoken. Other activities are less direct, but regardless of whether psychological safety is the main dish, it's always how I want to set the table.

People who don't feel that emotional safety are more likely to disengage and withhold their best work and ideas from their team because they feel they need to protect themselves. They circle the wagons, take no chances, and stick with what's worked so far. This is the version of safety that stifles ideas. People will always gravitate toward safety. But safety is a paradox. It's what allows us to grow, yet we can only grow by giving it up. The trick is to cultivate the sort of safety that opens up possibilities instead of the kind that shuts them down. All too often safety can melt into stagnation without our even noticing. A little danger is one way to shake loose from the numb passivity of too much safety.

The next chapter is all about cultivating that kind of danger.

HABIT BUILDER

Learn for Five Minutes

A good friend of mine is a high-powered exec at a major media empire. "As my career progressed and I moved up the hierarchy, I started seeing a kind of management tunnel vision where leaders forget how hard everyone else's job is. When you have power, it gets easy to wave people away and say, 'Just get it done.'"

So each January, instead of a New Year's resolution, she picks something new to learn for five minutes a day. There are mountains of simple apps you can get for free to learn languages, skills, and ideas. Over the years, she's tried knitting, Tai Chi, Swedish, coding. All of which were completely off-brand for her but gave her the chance to keep one foot in a beginner's mindset even as she tried to master the chosen task. Mastery, however, is not the point. "It keeps me very aware of how it feels to be lost, and how important it is to let people ask the questions they have and make the mistakes they need to make on their way to success. Plus, my kids got a bunch of nice lumpy knit hats."

When was the last time you let yourself try something completely new?

CHAPTER THREE

DANGER THAT THRILLS INSTEAD OF THREATENS

WE SPEND THE FIRST TEN YEARS OF OUR LIVES LEARNING TO READ DANGER SIGNALS AS PROM- ises. Hot stove? Back away, you will get burned. Stairs? Hold the rail or you will fall. (Of course, you spend many years seeing how close to the danger you can get without paying the consequences. "Maybe I can cut my own bangs!") That lesson of "Danger = Back Off" is critical to our continued survival as an individual and as a species. To be clear, I'm in favor of that lesson. But it's not always to our advantage. If you always shy away from where "there be dragons," how will you ever discover the richness, variety, and unexpected delights of the world? Yes, there is danger in exploring. But on the other side of the ocean there is cinnamon. There is Mozart. There are kangaroos. All sorts of surprises that will go undiscovered if we only stick with what we already know. Seeing the danger and choosing to sail off the map anyway is part of our human heritage. How else did the map get made in the first place?

This chapter is about developing a sense for the right kind of danger to employ—a danger that is about discovery rather than damage. Safe danger is not about causing people emotional pain. This shouldn't hurt. In fact, it's the opposite: It should be proof that danger is a warning, not a promise. I've developed a set of five principles for safety and five principles for danger to help make sure that my activities disrupt and disorient but don't damage. I use these guardrails to help balance play and purpose in a way that can *helpfully* mess with our comfy patterns of thought.

MY FIVE PRINCIPLES OF SAFETY

TALENT AGNOSTIC

Create a level playing field so that everyone can be proud of what they create. Highlight intention more than invention. This isn't about being better or worse than someone else; it's about being yourself. This isn't a chance to show off; it's an invitation to show up.

LOW STAKES

Draw content from people that is specific to them and their story, but not intrusive or invasive. Highly personal, but low stakes, like the story of a first kiss or a rule they secretly like to break. Give people the bond of sharing their lives without the discomfort of feeling exposed.

DECLINE WITH DIGNITY

Offer a gracious way out. People should feel invited to participate but allowed to decide for themselves how they do so. They should not feel put on the spot and forced into a corner. The depth of their contribution needs to be their choice.

GIVE AND RECEIVE

Participants should walk away having received something useful but also feeling that they've given something to the others. They should feel both valued and valuable.

EVERYONE IS HEARD

Some people aren't comfortable taking up space. Others are all too comfortable. But a person's volume setting is not indicative of their value.

Don't ask for volunteers to share and don't pick a few select examples. Everyone creates and everyone shares. Everyone's voice is heard with equal time and respect.

MY FIVE PRINCIPLES OF DANGER

SKIN IN THE GAME

Trivia contests and scavenger hunts are fun. Workshops and lectures are informative. But they don't ask much of you personally. Activities should ask people to give of themselves in one way or another. This is not a cooking show, where you can sit back and watch someone else do the dicing. Everyone must add a piece of themselves to the moment. That's what makes it valuable. And scary.

MAKE THE FAMILIAR UNFAMILIAR

We live lives of shortcuts, assumptions, familiarities, and autopilot. How many of us have ever found ourselves already at home after a long day with no real memory of the commute? So, to remind ourselves of the subtleties of the world around us and give us the space to rethink that world, remove the wrapping of familiarity and let us look around with fresh eyes and open minds.

SEE THE FOREST *AND* THE TREES

Build connection at multiple levels: (1) a personal, self-reflective level, (2) a person-to-person level, and (3) the level of the group as a whole. It's how these three levels intertwine and build on each other that allows people to find the meaning they need to find in the session.

FACTS + FEELINGS

People connect in different ways, so help them find hidden commonalities. Maybe they both come from the same city. Or maybe they both love the same show. Whether they have facts or feelings in common, I want to surface as many facets of a topic as possible to open up as many points of contact as possible.

THE WHY BEHIND THE WHY

People know what they're comfortable sharing. It's the emotional equivalent of inviting us to sit on the front porch and have a lemonade. But I'm after more. I politely request a tour of the inside. Then they'll point out the things they're used to pointing out. My goal is to go one more level in. I'm not a nosy neighbor, rifling through their garbage, but I am curious why those wooden carvings on the wall have been given such pride of place. I want to hear the motivations, the drives, the stories. I'd like to understand their thinking.

STIRRED, NOT SHAKEN

People should never regret our time together. This isn't emotional boot camp. I'm not trying to break them down and I'm not trying to fix them up. The kind of danger I'm after is just enough to give people second thoughts, but not so much that they walk out. Just enough to make the things we take for granted visible for a time. Whether it's "I never thought of that," "I never thought of it like that," or "I love being reminded of that" doesn't matter.

People rarely remember what you say for very long, but they do remember how you made them feel. I want them to feel unlocked. That can mean emotionally, intellectually, or socially, depending on the activity. But the point is I want them to feel a sense of openness, and I want them to feel a sense of ownership over that openness.

That's why safe danger is such a useful principle—it shows you believe in them. You're putting them in danger, acknowledging that danger, but giving them ownership by showing that you believe they can handle it. It makes me think about teaching a kid to ride a bike. They could fall down. Danger. But you're there with them. Safety. If they fall, you pick them up, clean them off, and make them try again. You don't do it for them the way you once might have tied their shoes or cut their meat when it proved too challenging; here you can't. They have to get back on. So then when they do get the feel for it, they know two things: They did it themselves, and you believed that they could.

My activities are obviously not iconic life experiences as learning to ride a bike—not by a long shot—but the core dynamic is there. A mild, voluntary danger that they need to confront on their own while you cheer from the sidelines. And the core takeaway is also there: They took a risk and it was worth it. In our case, the risk is transgressing the lines of professionalism, privacy, posturing, and so forth. It's the risk of being seen differently from now on. That's both the risk and the reward.

At first blush, it may seem that the "danger" only comes from making people uncomfortable. But that's just the first level. The danger I'm really after comes later. It comes in the walking away or the retelling of the story or the lying in bed and realizing that you have the means to change some element of your life. That's the danger: that you liked the idea of going down a new path. The real danger comes when you realize you have a choice to feel differently.

UNLOCK YOUR TALENT, THEN LOCK IT DOWN

Every offsite or all-hands meeting I've ever attended has started with the leader saying something along the lines of, "Our biggest asset is our talented people." Everyone tries to hire the best they can. But again and again I've seen organizations stacked with talent going untapped, not getting all the value they're paying for. Their people are only partially invested, scanning the field for their next career move. Between the direct costs of recruitment, lost productivity, lost institutional knowledge, extra burden on colleagues, training costs, lost time, and the risk of mis-hires, employee attrition is incredibly expensive and inefficient. If you've got great talent, you want to be (1) getting their best (2) for as long as possible.

When I was making things more difficult for myself, I had a teacher who would say, "You're eating soup with your hands." I feel like this would be an apt response to most team-building activities. They use up people's time without delivering anything of lasting meaning. Happy hours just aren't going to cut it. I'm positive I'm not the only one who has spent a happy hour listening to people whisper about job interviews. But activities that deliver safe danger actually help unlock a workforce and build community in a way that just doesn't happen with more familiar approaches to team building. These activities are a cheap, fun, and effective way to help keep good talent.

The fact is, when it comes to how most of us allocate our time, the urgent often eclipses the important. I hear again and again that the people and activities that truly matter take second place to pressing deadlines, looming meetings, and time-sensitive projects. People can't find the line between self-care and self-indulgence. Today's lunchtime walk gets pushed to next week so you can polish the big presentation. This week's call with a friend gets pushed to next quarter because the report is due and you're way behind. Your team's talent development gets bumped to next year because your bonuses depend on a strong quarter end and you need all hands on deck 24/7. This is a theme that I see across all the sectors and levels I work with, from C-suites to call centers, and it doesn't get better with seniority or salary. Constant urgency creates a short-term mindset, where self-care is consistently pushed to the bottom of the to-do list. It's often not even a nice-to-have but more like a nice-to-imagine.

That's why, if these activities resonate with you, it's worth the effort to carve out time to do them. Because if you ever want to make progress on what matters to you, you have to refuse to let *their* urgent eclipse *your* important.

Will my activities work for every single person in every

"I wish I'd spent more time in meetings."

single organization? The only thing that will work for every single person is oxygen. Beyond that, you're always going to find that some things click with some people better than with others. But what I will say is that, time and again, I've heard from people who thought this wouldn't work for them, their team, their company, their culture, but it did. People are hungry to connect, even if they don't know it. Who among us hasn't realized that they're starving until they smell dinner in the oven?

DELICATE DISRUPTION

People love, love, love to talk about thinking out of the box. Blue-sky thinking. But it's not enough to simply announce the intention to scrub off old mindsets. It takes effort. It's like soap. It's mechanical. It can't do its job without effort from you.

The proverbial box that everyone wants to think outside of is tricky because it can be so hard to identify. Conventional thinking is a slippery set of arbitrary rules, learned behaviors, and patterns of thought, all wrapped up with a bow made of the roles we've agreed to play. It's like the old fish in water joke: There are these two young fish swimming along and they happen to meet an older fish swimming the other way who nods at them and says, "Morning, kids. How's the water?" And the two young fish swim on for a bit, and then eventually one of them looks over at the other and goes, "What the heck is water?"

So, if you want to leave the box behind, the first step is to do the work of finding the box itself. What are the seams of your assumptions? Where are the edges of your sense of self?

If you're looking to chart a new course for yourself, then it's safe to say you're probably carrying a lot of stuff (such as behaviors, habits, defenses) that have been obscuring your vision. It's also probably safe to say that you're probably pretty familiar with all that stuff. Perhaps you know it so well you're not even sure where to draw the line between what makes you and what's holding you back. A little safe danger is a gentle way to begin to draw that line.

Whether the goals are in the personal realm (balance, confidence, purpose) or the professional arena (better, faster, cheaper), when it comes to change, the typical approach is to tackle this head-on with productivity apps, collaboration exercises, innovation training, sprints, scrums, speakers, lectures, worksheets, offsites, roundtables, panels, New Year's resolutions, and the like.

Those work on many levels for many people. But I've also heard many people complain about the degree of performance or superficiality involved. Applying new beliefs and behaviors on top of all the established elements of who you've always been and how you've always lived is rarely something you can just decide to do. That's why, so often after the initial boost, the impact of that approach can fade. You gain the weight back or the team stops communicating. I prefer more of an inside-out approach. An approach that is more likely to change the choices you make when no one is looking.

The things we typically focus on are more symptom than source. Yes, sometimes you do indeed want to focus on symptoms—cold medicine so you can sleep, crutches so you can walk. But that approach leaves the underlying cause intact. If you want it to change, you need to go deeper. You need to heal what's broken so that you don't face those symptoms again. (Also, frankly, addressing just the symptoms can often mask the source until it becomes toxic.) So, rather than focusing directly on a symptom, I prefer to aim for what may be beneath it.

That's why, when I want to affect concrete outcomes like productivity, collaboration, and loyalty, I focus on the more amorphous inputs that create the best conditions for those results. The inputs may feel off target and even fluffy—but they are in fact harder to get to because they deal with experience. People tend to think that, if we understand what an experience is supposed to teach, then we know it. "I get it, I get it, move on." We think this, even though we have plenty of evidence from our daily lives that there's a chasm of difference between when someone *tells* us what we should be doing (exercise more, drink less, watch cholesterol, practice gratitude, don't sweat the small stuff, floss) and the moment we're expected to do it ourselves. There's an experiential element to learning that cannot be skipped

"Out of the way—I binge-watched E.R. over the weekend!"

if you want to build the new neural pathways that unlock new skills. I can have you read books about buoyancy and Michael Phelps, but that doesn't mean you can swim. Until you've gotten your feet wet and experienced it in your body, you're never going to get to Marco Polo or cliff diving. You're going to miss out because you've got a terrible teacher who isn't focusing on the fundamentals. Fundamentals like getting your face wet, like blowing bubbles. Fundamentals that feel off target and even fluffy but that actually develop the behaviors and intuitions you need to excel.

This is why the safe danger dynamic is so useful. It creates a small moment, an emotional microcosm, for people to experience what they've been missing or avoiding and test out how it feels to be vulnerable, to fail, to trust, to be generous. Unblinking Line (see page 126) lets people remember what it feels like to focus on something without demanding perfection. Childhood Hoodwinks (see page 204) reminds us of the pitfalls of our own assumptions. Blobviously (see page 201) reminds us that ours is not the only way to see a problem or a solution. As I said, these are all experiences in miniature, but like a sample tray outside a café, you get a taste and then get to choose for yourself if you're willing to pay the price for more.

If you want to spark change in yourself or your team, start by building the kind of safety that stimulates people's voices rather than stifles them and balance that with the kind of danger that helps people feel exhilarated instead of exposed. It's in the overlap of these two feelings that you can help people experience and practice the qualities that make a difference.

I've been lucky enough to work with and be guided by people who have done the hard work of finding their voice and using it to make the world a more interesting place. Each chapter in the next part delves into one of the powerful qualities I've seen them use to bring out the best in themselves and their teams: joy, vulnerability, curiosity, optimism, connection, trust, and creativity. I've seen these qualities deliver profits and reveal purpose. For people who want to change how they show up in their personal or professional life, safe danger can unlock those qualities and help you change your workplace, community, and home.

HABIT BUILDER

Random Dining

When I was a kid I had an uncle who loved leaving the small choices to chance. Uncle Herb was a wild-haired impressionist painter, and he went through a phase where, whenever we would go out to eat, he would always just pick the third thing on the menu. The third sandwich, the third ice cream flavor, the third cocktail. Whatever was on offer, he'd just pick the third one. Sometimes it was boring or disappointing, but then he'd talk about what was missing or off and we'd discuss what we liked and why. But, of course, plenty of times he'd come across a surprise gem he never would have picked for himself. He said it was totally worth all the disappointments to discover this new treasure.

Try it for a week and see what you discover. Pick the third pizza on the menu. The third sandwich bread on the shelf. The third coffee from the list. Let a little randomness expand your palate.

PART II

TO BOOST QUALITY, FOCUS ON QUALITIES

CHAPTER FOUR

TO ACCELERATE PRODUCTIVITY, INSPIRE JOY

DON'T DISMISS DELIGHT

People love joy, but they don't respect it. Especially on weekdays. Joy is an indulgence most people struggle to justify ("I know it's silly, don't judge me!"), apologize for spending on ("I couldn't help myself!"), and fail to make time for ("Sorry, I'm swamped!"). Joy is for when you pause real life—weekends, vacations, stolen moments. And that's certainly a popular way to look at it. Not a very healthy way, but a popular one.

When it comes to our professional life, we're accustomed to draining all the color from the experience and looking at cold, hard facts—not warm, fuzzy feelings. We want to be taken seriously, so we take work seriously. The idea of taking joy seriously is hard for many people to wrap their heads around, because you risk looking frivolous, flaky, immature. You risk the reputation you've carefully cultivated at home and work. You risk that awful feeling of being judged. But what I've seen is that embracing joy leads to exactly the sort of life and achievements worth admiring.

Your joy and your job are not enemies. For most people, these two are just in a dysfunctional relationship, like siblings who each feel they need to steal time from the other. Our jobs belittle joy, and joy throws up its arms and abandons the job to its unhappy fate. But the healthy version of their relationship looks very different. When these two elements of your life collaborate, jobs can focus joy and joy can fuel jobs.

This is not to say that joy instantly makes everything easy. The difference is you don't mind the difficulty so much. Work and effort are not the same thing. When I use the word *work*, I'm not talking jobs, careers, professions. I mean unfun effort. Work is Effort + Resistance. Work gets you wishing you could be somewhere else, doing something else, with someone else, all wrapped in the urge to procrastinate or call in sick. Effort is not the problem, though. Look at play. Play is Effort + Joy. It's not easy to learn to tango, master a chessboard, or restore a hot rod. Yet, we enjoy the effort.

In fact, one secret to boosting personal and professional productivity, inspiration, and engagement is to take work out of the equation—shift the experience from Effort + Resistance to Effort + Joy.

EFFORT + JOY

There's a famous aphorism (variously attributed to everyone from Mark Twain to Confucius) that says, "Do what you love and you'll never work a day in your life." Although this makes for a delightful bumper sticker, the fact is most people haven't ended up in lives that perfectly align with their heart's bliss. Even those of us lucky enough to be in our chosen fields undoubtedly breathe a sigh a relief when Friday finally arrives. So, what to do? Many people put their nose to the grindstone, push through, lean in, make the best of it. After all, no one said life would be a picnic.

But a job doesn't have to feel like work. That's an expectation, not a requirement. They say misery loves company; well, so does joy. If you're able to make your workplace a happy place, if you're able to infuse your relationships, your community, your family with joy and play, you'll be nourishing a foundation that changes the tone of everything that's built on top of that base.

Of course, if it were just that easy, this would be a very different world. But it is possible. I know because I've seen the impact Effort + Joy can make. And so have you.

Everything from weight loss to language learning and bill paying has had a gamified element added to it, where you get a score and then try to beat your score the next week. Cars with Eco Mileage that compare your driving to the average, subtly encouraging you to drive more economically. Trash cans with basketball hoops. Practice drills and game day both entail exertion and persistence, but in one context it's tedious and in another it's thrilling. The effort remains, but it's transmuted from Effort + Resistance to Effort + Joy, because you want to be doing the thing. This is more than just a spoonful of sugar to make the medicine go down. It's not masking the pain; it's replacing it.

FUEL FOR THOUGHT

You might assume that a chain of roadside gas and grocery stores might not be too invested in the people they hire to pump the gas or stock the chips. But QuikTrip took an unconventional approach and invested time and money in making sure its people are happy, have a sense of purpose, and feel valued. The homepage announces, "We are a fast-paced happy bunch that provides great customer service while selling food, snacks, and gasoline to a diverse base of hungry, thirsty, and gasoline needy customers!" Happy. With an exclamation point. That's what a roadside convenience mart leads with. This is a sector where customers and employees have little choice. You're out of gas, you go to the first gas station you can. You're hungry, it's a place for a snack. You need a job, it's a place for a paycheck. It's not a place for comparison shopping. Yet, *happy* is what it chooses to value. And the company has thrived (and profited) because of it. In an industry with an average turnover rate of 109 percent, Quik-Trip's is 13 percent. With a thousand stores and valued at $11 billion, QuikTrip's headline to describe itself is, "A Company Created to Provide Opportunities for Employees to Grow and Succeed."

Is this a fluke? A one-off? We're generally socialized to see happiness as a nice-to-have once you've got all your other ducks in a row. But the research shows that happier ducks are better at lining up.

JOY IS PRODUCTIVE

Joy is a productivity powerhouse. An overwhelming body of evidence shows that people work harder when they're happy.

We'll start with quantity. An in-depth, long-term study of seven hundred people by the University of Warwick Department of Economics in England found that employees who were happy at work outperformed their less joyful colleagues in especially demanding tasks by a whopping 12 percent (that's like saving a whole hour in your workday).[1] Gallup's State of the Global Workplace report found that engaged employees were 17 percent more productive overall, and companies with the highest rates of employee engagement were 21 percent more profitable.[2] A study published in the *Journal of Applied Psychology* found that people in a good mood are 31 percent more productive than those in a neutral or bad mood.[3] One study showed that a portfolio of companies ranked in the top 10 percent for employee satisfaction outperformed those in the bottom 10 percent by 2.3 percent to 3.8 percent annually in stock returns.[4] These productivity surges can be chalked up to a range of factors influenced by happiness, including heightened motivation, enhanced engagement, and increased creativity.

What about quality? The study revealed that happier employees use time more effectively, increase their pace without sacrificing quality, commit fewer errors, and demonstrate greater focus and accuracy. Meanwhile, unhappy workers are more susceptible to distractions and make more mistakes.

Happy employees mean less turnover, fewer mistakes, more productivity, and increased profit. So, what's the problem? Business leaders have been well trained in the importance of driving results, achieving growth, and increasing profits. But the field is far less educated on the role that happiness plays in achieving those goals. Often the people who hold the purse strings are so focused on the purse that they miss the point of the strings—to open up that purse to spend on things that will fill the purse even more.

Although salary is obviously important, it is rarely cited as the key reason employees feel happy, satisfied, or engaged at work.[5] With the competition for top talent intensifying, more and more companies are pouring resources into more emotionally intelligent perks aimed at enhancing employee satisfaction. In fact, according to the professors who ran the Warwick study, Google's employee satisfaction rate rose by an incredible 37 percent after the company invested more in employee support.[6] But having an impact does not require a Google-size budget. One simple experiment showed that by spending two dollars per person on chocolates and fruit, productivity increased by 20 percent for a short period of time.[7] Now, to be very clear, I believe happiness takes more than an occasional fruit basket, but it's telling to see such a direct correlation between joy and productivity.

WHY JOY IS PRODUCTIVE

Okay, so joy makes people more productive. Why? Is it all the whistling while they work? Not so much. Turns out that joy has a major impact on our brain and body, and this is why Effort + Joy, as opposed to Effort + Resistance, leads to the increased quality and quantity of our output.

MORE BRAIN POWER

An internal global study by Merck, a German multinational science and technology company (a sector not necessarily known for its rollicking playful nature), found that joy has a major impact on people's ability to analyze the world around them, absorb new information, and find new ways to use that information.[8]

Joy primes the brain for peak performance. When we feel anxious our adrenaline spikes and our attention narrows. But happiness floods the brain with dopamine, serotonin, and endorphins, chemicals that not only enhance mood but also play pivotal roles in cognitive functions, motivation, and focus. When we're in a positive emotional state, the prefrontal cortex, responsible for higher-order cognitive functions, operates more efficiently; so we're less likely to think in terms of rigid categories. That makes us more creative and allows for more adaptive thinking, creative problem-solving, and a willingness to explore different approaches.

Positive emotions also help maintain a balance in stress hormones such as cortisol by reducing overall stress levels, improving cognitive function, and leading to better decision-making.

On top of helping our brain work better, happiness also helps our brain grow. Positive emotions facilitate neuroplasticity—the brain's ability to reorganize and form new neural connections—which supports learning, adaptation, and the development of more efficient cognitive pathways.

MORE ACCEPTING

Our brain evolved to protect us. One of the basic ways it does that is by drawing a line between us and anything that's not us. But now that we're not looking over our shoulder for big bad wolves, some of that hardwired paranoia has lost its relevance. For example, it's scientifically documented that people recognize faces of their own race faster than faces of different races.[9] But happiness seems to help with that. It's been shown that this facial bias is significantly lower when we're in a state of joy.[10] We're physiologically more open to different kinds of people when we feel safe and happy.

MORE PERSISTENT

Happiness fosters intrinsic motivation, making individuals more driven to pursue tasks for the inherent joy the tasks bring. As a result, happier people have been shown to exhibit greater resilience in the face of challenges, which enables them to bounce back from setbacks, fight through obstacles, and maintain productivity in the long run.

MORE CONNECTED

Good workplace relationships are a cornerstone of employee happiness and productivity. A survey conducted by the Society for Human Resource Management reported that 77 percent of employees feel that good relationships with colleagues make them more productive at work.[11] Positive emotions are associated with stronger social bonds and a sense of belonging, social support that reduces stress and enhances people's sense of well-being.

THE JOYLESS CLUB

But even with all this evidence pouring in, organizations are still struggling to act on it. Ninety-two percent of executives agree that high employee engagement leads to happier customers, yet only 37 percent of executives strongly agree that engagement is a significant organizational focus.[12]

Meanwhile, research from Gallup found that two-thirds of employees are disengaged at work; 50 percent of employees consider meetings wasted time; 58 percent of employees say complacent leadership is the top reason they feel disengaged; and 80 percent of employees say meaningful learning and development opportunities would help them feel more engaged on the job. The study also found that the majority of the world's employees are quiet quitting, which is when someone is completely checked out. As Gallup says, "They may be physically present or logged into their computer, but they don't know what to do or why it matters, and lack any supportive bonds with their coworkers, boss or their organization." Nearly six in ten employees fell into this category.[13]

Knowing this, it may not be as shocking as it should be that across the countries and areas Gallup surveyed, over half of currently employed employees are watching for or actively seeking a new job. Naturally, more money is on everyone's wish list, but surprisingly it's not the thing most people flagged as a reason for a job hunt. When asked, "If you could make one change at your current employer to make it a great place to work, what would it be?" only 28 percent said pay and benefits. A whopping 57 percent focused on employee engagement, well-being, or workplace culture. They come for the paycheck, but they'll stay for the people—and a culture that not only supports joy but also invests in it.

The statistics show that leaders who nourish a joyful culture that fosters psychological safety can create a work environment of increased productivity

"Great job everyone. But next quarter I want to see twenty percent higher returns and fifteen percent less joy."

and profitability where employees feel valued, engaged, and motivated to do their best work.

So, why don't they all do it?

I've noticed that when I speak with experts in workplace behaviors such as HR and talent professionals, they are 100 percent on board with these revelations. Likewise, when I speak with C-suite leaders, they get it. It is almost self-evident to these two levels that a healthy, happy workplace affects every area of business. The levels where I find the most resistance are the midtier managers—not because they are monsters who believe that fear and pressure are the only ways to motivate people (well, not all of them). It's about priorities. They are usually working with limited resources and constrained budgets and need to be sure that the time and money they spend will have a worthwhile return on investment (ROI). In our culture, the urgent tends to eclipse the important. What do you prioritize when the budget is tight? Managers may know that a happy, healthy team will do better work but feel like now is just not the time to focus on that. It's hard to get past the stigma of frivolity. "You used your budget for *what*? Now is no time for fun! Now is the time to roll up the sleeves, stiffen the upper lip, get it done, because otherwise we'll all be polishing our résumés."

Budget holders often see joy as a nice-to-have when times are very good. A reward. From what I've seen, though, I'd suggest the opposite is true. It's when things are tightest and toughest and people are the most squeezed that you need your best people to be at their best.

DON'T BLAME COVID

Many leaders I speak with lament the impact the pandemic has had on their corporate culture. The argument goes: "This is all COVID's fault. The pandemic disrupted the normal flow of work life and now people are scattered and that's why they feel so disconnected and discontented. If we can just get them all back in the office, it will fix itself."

That's an easy argument to make. Easy, and wrong. If it were accurate, then people who were fully back in the office would be the most engaged. But that's not the case. Surveys show that hybrid and remote employees are actually more engaged than on-site employees.[14] So, yes, COVID did disrupt the status quo. But in many ways that was actually a helpful thing because it revealed that engagement is much more about *how* people feel than where they feel it. In fact, Gallup found that people's relationships with their team, managers, and leadership actually have almost four times as much influence on their stress load as whether they're remote or on-site.

Illness is an apt metaphor. If you get a cold, it's not the cold virus's fault. Your cold actually reveals a weakened immune system (stress, lack of sleep) or carelessness (touching public surfaces) or dangerous local elements (children are basically walking Petri dishes). Same with this. Gartner's research shows that 82 percent of employees say it's important that their organizations see them as a whole person, but only 45 percent feel seen that way.[15] People aren't feeling disconnected just because the system was disrupted; those feelings are a symptom of a system that has neglected the things that keep us healthy and happy. The disruption just allowed us to feel it more clearly.

IT'S NOT YOUR JOB'S JOB TO MAKE YOU HAPPY

The ask to prioritize joy and connection in the workplace can certainly feel impractical and out of place in a world of deadlines, performance reviews, and shareholder reports. It's easier (and more familiar) to *tell* people to suck it up and do their job than it is to show up for them in a way that makes them *want* to do it. Easier. Faster. Cheaper. In the short term. Thus, many people simply feel that employers are responsible for paychecks, not happiness.

Maybe they're not. But it does certainly seem to be in their interest to be concerned with workforce happiness.

Organizations that recognize and invest in fostering happiness in the workplace are not only contributing to the well-being of their employees but also reaping the quantifiable rewards of a more productive and efficient workforce. A study in the *Harvard Business Review* found that organizations with a strong emphasis on employee experience make four times the average profit of those that do not prioritize the well-being of their workforce.[16] (They were also almost 25 percent smaller, which suggests even higher levels of productivity and innovation.)

I've seen the impact when employers create the circumstances that encourage joy and remove obstacles that dampen it. I'm not talking about party hats and confetti drops every ten minutes. I'm talking about understanding what motivates your employees as human beings, considering their personal values, aspirations, and individual needs, and helping them thrive both in the workplace and at home.

That said, it's not just up to the HR department to create a happy workplace culture. Everyone has a role to play in creating a positive work environment. It's up to leaders to create a psychologically safe space where staff feel comfortable speaking up, asking questions, taking educated risks, and not fearing making mistakes. It's up to every employee to contribute to a culture of positivity, respect, and collaboration.

JOY IS A FLAVOR OF HAPPINESS

Obsolete leadership mindsets aren't the only issue keeping joy at a minimum. After all, even if your boss is a heartless crab, that doesn't mean you can't take action on your own. And yet, startlingly few people do just that. Why? Often the biggest obstacle to bringing more joy to our lives is ourselves.

Ingrid Fetell Lee has spent almost her entire career thinking about, designing for, and exploring joy.[17] Specifically, how do we get more of it?

Her wonderful book *Joyful* was a *New York Times* best seller, her TED Talk has been watched more than three million times (and counting), and her workshops and speaking engagements are legendary for their simple, powerful insights and pointers.

Fetell Lee's personal and professional mission is to help people get more joy into their lives. So she felt like the perfect person for me to ask about why it's so hard to do just that.

"Ha! Good question!" She laughed. "First of all, it's important to note that I see joy and happiness as two distinct things."

Fetell Lee explains that, whereas joy can be an element of happiness, joy is simpler and more immediate than happiness. She sees joy as an intense momentary experience of positive emotion. Something that makes you smile. Makes you laugh. Joy is often associated with experiences that are vivid, playful, and exuberant. It can be sparked by simple, sensory-rich experiences such as seeing bright colors, experiencing a sense of wonder, or engaging in playful activities. Joy is often felt in the present moment and can be fleeting. Joy is about the little things, the day-to-day pleasures and surprises that give us energy and connect us to other people. A hug from a friend you run into by chance. A moment of quiet cuddling with a pet. A cluster of balloons tied to a fire escape. The first bite of the first summer peach. That's joy.

She describes happiness, on the other hand, as a more enduring and overall state of well-being and contentment. It encompasses a broader range of emotions and life satisfaction. Happiness is influenced by various factors such as relationships, personal fulfillment, and a sense of purpose. Unlike joy, which can be sparked by specific experiences, happiness tends to be more stable and long-lasting.

Although I've used the two interchangeably throughout this chapter so far, that's because common usage treats them that way, and much of the research I've cited focuses on the broader term *happiness*. But I've deliberately made this chapter about joy. Why? Joy obviously can lead to happiness. But joy is both more accessible and more impactful. Joy can be found in simple, everyday experiences and objects, which makes it easier to control than happiness, since happiness may be influenced by external circumstances or life events.

Joy doesn't need to be a permanent state of being—in fact, it can't be—which lowers the bar for entry and expectations. Joyful experiences can serve as sources of resilience during challenging times when happiness is elusive. You don't need to be dancing in the streets all day and your office doesn't need to be a scene out of a Bollywood dance climax. But you can add a pop of color, an element of play, and make a difference in your day.

BARRIERS TO JOY

One of the important things to remember is that joy is not something that happens to you. Like all the feelings we have, joy may be triggered by something external, but it comes from us. It's already in you, sitting around, just waiting for the experience that will set it free and let it shine. But, though joy may be within reach, it can still be hard to grasp. Why? According to Fetell Lee, because of three main barriers to finding more joy.

AWARENESS

Many people don't even really know what brings them joy. They go through the motions of what they're told *should* make them happy, but the spark is missing. "They just haven't felt joy in a really long time, so they don't know how to find their way back," she said.

So, the first step to reconnecting with joy is to set habit aside and become aware of the kinds of things that genuinely make you feel joyful.

TIME AND SPACE

One of the most frequent objections Fetell Lee hears is some form of, "I don't have time to do the things that bring me joy."

"That's a result of an all-or-nothing perspective," Fetell Lee said. But joy doesn't need to be a grand gesture. In fact, it often comes in small, simple moments. Maybe it's the new lamp that brings a pop of joyful color to your desk or watching a puppy jump for soap bubbles.

"I was once helped by a nurse who had decorated her badge with multicolored medication vial tops that she'd hot-glued together into a little rosette.

The hospital was endless gray and beige as far as your eye could see, until it landed on this colorful little joyful creation." If you're feeling squeezed for bandwidth, start by giving yourself small moments of joy in your day even if it's just a vibrant plant or happy yellow coffee mug.

PERMISSION

Permission is especially tricky because it encompasses both internal and external permissions. External is the easiest to spot. It's a workplace where everyone stops chatting and looks busy when the boss walks by. It's a family where the unconventional is unacceptable. It's a friend group that ridicules anything that doesn't conform. Outside forces say, "No."

Internal is more pernicious. Fetell Lee describes this situation as: "I know what brings me joy. I could do it, but for some reason I can't seem to give myself permission to do it." And although we all have our own issues, Fetell Lee has noticed some consistent patterns and has created a rogues' gallery of the seven main mindsets that may be causing you to withhold permission for enjoying life more thoroughly. She calls them the Killjoys.

THE KILLJOYS

INNER CRITIC

"What will people think of me?"

Inner Critic is that judgy voice in your head that says the things you like are stupid, weird, or embarrassing. It thinks it's protecting you from ridicule, but it's actually cheating you out of what you love in an effort to earn other people's approval. It feeds on your fear of judgment.

TASKMASTER

"I haven't earned it yet."

Taskmaster believes your value is defined by your output, so it says joy is a reward that's only allowed after you put in the hard work. Unfortunately, this is also the mindset that never feels you've put in enough work because Taskmaster secretly believes that you don't really deserve joy.

PERFECTIONIST

"I can't have a dinner party until I get new napkins."

Perfectionist doesn't allow you joy until everything is perfect. If "perfect" seems out of reach, Perfectionist tells you not to even bother trying. Its version of success depends on what other people think, so Perfectionist puts the power in the hands of everyone but you.

NERVOUS NELLY

"I'm not going to try that new restaurant because I wouldn't know what to order."

Nervous Nelly is terrified of loss and disappointment and will do anything to protect you from them. It never wants to leave the safety of the comfort zone. As with many of the Killjoys, it's a valid self-preservation tool that has grown so big it blocks out the light of all other possibilities.

CONTROL FREAK

"If I'm not careful, they'll all laugh at me."

Control Freak is afraid of letting loose. It's afraid that if you get caught up in a moment of joy, you'll let down your guard and reveal those awkward, uncool parts of yourself. Control Freak feels that love and acceptance depend on being "normal." It is on a mission to save you from the total humiliation of being yourself.

GREEN-EYED MONSTER

"I'm never going to get to take a trip as great as theirs."

Green-Eyed Monster believes there's only so much joy to go around. If someone else gets it, there's less for you. Green-Eyed Monster is stuck in a life of envious comparison, which makes it hard to both celebrate other people's successes and appreciate all that you yourself already have.

PROTECTIVE PESSIMIST

"I'm sure I won't win."

Protective Pessimist thinks it's protecting you from the pain of disappointment by lowering your expectations. It sees hope as naive and is so focused on what's probably going to go wrong that it blocks you from enjoying what's going right.

ANTI-KILLJOYS

The policies and consequences of an organization like a school, community, or company obviously exist outside of you. External permissions can change as you graduate, relocate, or take a new job. Internal permission is different. All that internal judgment will follow you through all those outside changes. The expectations, the fear of consequences get so internalized that the external forces don't even need to act because we police ourselves.

"And you call yourself an inner critic, you pathetic loser?"

So, how do we push back on these Killjoys when the voices of judgment are so familiar we think they're our own? First, by recognizing that they're not our own. That's where safe danger can play a role. It's a technique that can help create some distance between you and those voices so that you have space for some anti-Killjoys.

LOVE YOUR FRENEMIES

Joy and Killjoys aren't enemies. Not really. The Killjoys holding you back aren't trying to squash your joy; they're trying to keep you safe. Joy is collateral damage. They're misguided, but they're not malicious. In fact, if you listen to them, they'll lead you right to the joy you've been missing out on.

INSIDE OUT

Being kind to ourselves is ironically one of the hardest things to do. Other people may forgive us, but we can find all sorts of reasons that we don't deserve to give ourselves a break. We can be far more kind to others than to ourselves. So, that's a behavior we can build on: If you find it hard to let yourself off the hook, start by practicing on others.

Fetell Lee said that one surefire way to identify your own Killjoys is to pay attention to how you judge others: Why is she wearing that? Who does he think he is, hoping to win that award? She looks ridiculous dancing like that. Oh, taking a break already?

"We look at other people and we have judgments of them. That often means we hold the same judgment of ourselves," she said. Her suggestion is to pay close attention when we think things like that, and try turning it inside out: Wow, she looks like she's having fun. Wow, he's really going after what he wants. Wow, she looks so free. I'd like to be that free.

By rewriting your internal scripts, you begin to give yourself permission to do it yourself. Every time you catch yourself judging and instead give someone else permission, you're actually giving yourself a little more permission.

MAKING FRIENDS WITH THE OPPOSITE

A lot of times, the way to quiet a Killjoy is to make friends with its opposite, with the very thing it's trying to protect you from. Ready to leave Nervous Nelly behind? Introduce her to what she fears: disappointment. Brace yourself, and get your hopes up. Maybe start small. Expect a new restaurant to be delicious. Maybe it will be. But if it's not, let yourself feel disappointed. This isn't easy. You've built this killjoy to protect you from disappointment, and for good reason. It hurts to be disappointed, judged, abandoned.

So, that's why you don't need to get rid of the Killjoys completely. This isn't about erasing those voices entirely; it's just about lowering their volume to an appropriate level. All the killjoy feelings are there for a purpose, but often they're like overgrown emotional vines that are choking the life out of everything else. A little healthy pruning is good for everything in the garden.

FINDING THE FORGOTTEN

We all leave a trail of beloved memories behind us as we move through our lives, and the opportunity to retrieve and relive them can flood us with a sudden nostalgic dopamine rush, an emotional endorphin boost that reignites our hearts, our curiosity, our purpose.

These are more than just nice memories that we've misplaced. They're buried treasure chests, full of the sort of riches that can make a whole new life possible. These are inspiring, energizing parts of ourselves that can drive the engines of joy and purpose and make us look forward to waking up, make us toe-tappingly impatient to get started, so absorb us that we lose track of time even though we're working harder than ever. These memories are our personal lists of what makes life worth living.

Sometimes it just takes a little reminder to help you find your way back to what you've lost. That's a little of what I try to do with safe danger activities: use them as emotional breadcrumbs to help people find the parts of themselves they may have misplaced in all the stress and pressure of careers and romance and life. Often it just takes the little nudge of recalling specifics. The smell of summer sunblock when you're digging a hole at the beach, the texture of your stuffed animal's ear, the call that you'd gotten the job, made the team, won the award.

For me it was, ironically, "Don't You Forget About Me," the song by O.M.D. from the *Pretty in Pink* soundtrack. I'd completely forgotten about it. I was in a car on the way to the airport in Chicago after a full-day workshop, and that song came on and my heart suddenly just felt deeply, deeply happy. I couldn't stop the smile from spreading from my face to my toes. Though I hadn't thought about it in decades, I discovered in that moment that it still plucked the same chords in my heart that it had when I was a teenager listening to it as I sat on the worn green vinyl seats of the morning school bus.

You can force yourself to smile. But you can't force yourself to feel it. That authentic joy has to come on its own. What you can do is make room for it; welcome it; nurture it. Respect it. When I design activities, I want people to refamiliarize themselves with their joy so they can find their own way back to it on their own in their own career and personal life.

We tend to think of joy as light and easy, but there are plenty of times when a moment of joy brings up resistance. Some part of us wants to feel the joy, but another just won't let it in. This might look like habitually reaching for your phone in a joyful moment, seeking distraction from the joy.

It might mean faultfinding—looking for problems when things are good. It might mean bracing and being on guard for loss. Fetell Lee points out, "Noticing your habitual strategies for dampening joy can ultimately help you find more of it."

One of my favorite activities for doing just that is called Hidden Joys.

ACTIVITY

Hidden Joys

There was an astronaut. A bottle of wine. A tire swing. Each the size of a hamster. Each made of white air-dry clay. Each hidden somewhere in plain sight around the office.

These were all artifacts of our Hidden Joys activity—an easy, playful way to tackle the three main obstacles to joy that Fetell Lee points out: awareness, time and space, and permission.

When I was at IDEO, we would often have visitors come to the studio and we'd give them a tour of our wildly decorated project rooms, unhinged creative experiments, and festively colorful makespace. But even with all this abundance of imaginative bells and whistles, it was our little café that held my favorite thing. Up high on the ceiling next to an unassuming air-conditioning duct was a little surprise: a perfectly legible, obvious but not ostentatious decal that read "99 percent of people will not notice this." I never pointed it out, but I could always tell the moment when someone spotted it. A smile would creep on their face and they would glance mischievously side to side at the people around them to see whether anyone else had noticed.

That little bit of surprise brought a rush of unexpected joy to people that I just loved. It's a quality that some of my favorite street artists also specialize in. For example, there's a French artist called Space Invader who uses mosaic tiles to add pixelated eighties video game characters to the walls of Paris. And what's magical about them is how, if you're just walking down a street, you might not ever notice them. But once you know to look for them, you start seeing them everywhere. And it feels like you've been brought into a secret conversation that no one around you realizes is happening.

In Germany there's an artist named Jan Vormann who finds crumbling facades and fixes them with Legos. These colorful pops of joy wait like a little wink for the initiated to give you a boost and put a smile on your face.

Hidden in Brooklyn's Prospect Park are little pint-sized "fairy doors" affixed to the base of random trees, with tiny door knobs and teeny peepholes. Some even have little laundry lines nearby or little bowls of food left over from a recent fairy picnic. These are just unexpected moments of whimsy gifted from one stranger to another.

I try to capture a little of this joyful magic in my Hidden Joys activity. Start by brainstorming twenty things that brought you joy at any stage of your life. Activities, places, things, food, music, and hobbies are all fair game. Pizza, Winnie-the-Pooh, swimming, cats, swimming cats, whatever. Maybe it's dancing till dawn or skydiving through the clouds, reading a good book with a slice of pizza or watching bad TV with a glass of wine. Whatever activity from whenever phase of life. What's your joy hall of fame?

Now take some air-dry clay, pick something joyful (you can use your hall of fame or come up with something completely different), and create a sculpture that represents that activity. A joy totem. (Don't stress about your artistic prowess. For most of us, clay is not our day job. Just do what you can. This is less about being anatomically correct and more about sharing the feeling of joy. Take your time. Express what you love.)

If you're doing this on your own, skip to the hiding part. But if you have the option of doing it with a group, everyone should take turns explaining their creation. This is a chance to get to know each other on a little more personal level and to see both what brings others joy and how they choose to depict it. As people share, you can ask follow-up questions like, "When was the last time you did *X*? What's your favorite part of your creation? What is it about *X* that brought you joy?"

A nice thing about the group dynamic is that your work can be inspiring for others. For example, one time we did this, someone's creation was about sunrises and it got me thinking about the last sunrise I watched—specifically, about how I couldn't remember the last one. So, guess what I did the next morning with a cup of coffee and a cat in my lap? You never know what your joy can spark in someone else—don't keep it to yourself.

Once your creation has dried, you're going to hide it somewhere in plain sight, but not easily seen. Maybe in the background of your Zoom calls, maybe nestled in a favorite plant, maybe atop the office fridge. The point is, it should be a discovery for your audience. An unlooked-for surprise. A little pop of joy.

But keep in mind that this is also, or maybe mostly, for you. It's a moment for you to wink at yourself, give yourself a gentle dopamine rush, or deliver a reminder to block off some time to go swimming with your cat at sunrise.

HIDDEN JOYS
Sparks of Surprise

Primary Quality
Joy

Supporting Themes
Community
Tactile Storytelling
Inspiration

The What
A two-part opportunity to celebrate the little things that have brought us joy throughout our lives.

The How

Reflect: First, everyone is asked to write down ten things that brought them joy at some stage of their life (including the present one). It can be an activity, a place, a thing, a food, music, a hobby, and so forth.

Create: In twenty-five minutes, everyone uses air-dry clay to create a simple sculpture that embodies the item from their joys list that means the most to them.

Share: Everyone takes turns sharing their sculpture and the story of its inspiration with the group. When every sculpture has been shared, everyone is asked to find a hiding place for theirs that is in plain sight, but not easily seen. Maybe it is positioned to appear in the background of video calls or maybe perched high on a window frame. The point is that spotting it should be a discovery, an unlooked-for surprise, a little pop of joy for whoever spots it.

The Why

Whether you do this remotely with colleagues or in the backyard with the neighbors, this is a chance for everyone to share something that has played a key role in their life and to see and be inspired by what brings joy to others. This is a moment for people to be vulnerable without feeling exposed. They can risk sharing something about themselves without actually facing any repercussions. Then, hiding it in plain sight is an opportunity to give others a gift of surprise, discovery, and joy. But as much as it is a reward for observant guests, it is also a moment for the creators to wink at themselves, remind themselves what brings them joy, generate a gentle dopamine rush, or give themselves a nudge to block off some future time for it on their busy calendars.

The Materials

Air-dry clay

JOY IS ENOUGH OF A REASON

Joy and work aren't enemies. Sure, miserable people can be plenty productive. But despite the established wisdom of stereotypes and clichés that says a productive mindset means facing facts and saying "playtime is over, get to work," the actual facts say otherwise. According to research, statistics, psychology, and profit reports, joy is actually a secret weapon that can supercharge the productivity of a classroom, a family, a career, a business.

Cultivating your personal, professional, or workplace's capacity for joy means that you'll both accomplish more and appreciate it more. Joy leads to productivity and feeling productive leads to joy. It's a virtuous circle.

But it takes practice.

Joy is one of the most powerful divining rods for locating your uniqueness. But many people have been trained to tune out listening to or for their joy, especially in any context beyond indulgence. That's why activities like Hidden Joys (see page 70), Conceptual Candies (see page 208), and Hour Gift to You (see page 223) are about delight for delight's sake, not making joy justify itself but celebrating its arrival on your doorstep and welcoming it in. Make space for joy so that it can settle in and infuse the rest of your efforts with its magic.

HABIT BUILDER

Celebrate the Little Victories

When leaders ask Ingrid Fetell Lee how to incorporate joy into the office without a large budget, she suggests celebrating the everyday victories. "Celebration doesn't need to be lavish," she says. "It can be a confetti toss."

As a way to bring more joy into your life, for one week try finding some small thing each day to celebrate in some small way. Answered that email that was hanging over your head all week? Give yourself five minutes of sitting outside in the sun. Finished your to-do list and still picked up the kids on time? Take five minutes for a family dance party. Didn't lose your cool when someone cut you off on the freeway? Reward yourself with a soft pair of fun-colored socks. Because why not wear fun-colored socks?

CHAPTER FIVE

TO PINPOINT PURPOSE, INSPIRE VULNERABILITY

LIGHTEN THE DARKNESS

My mother loved antiquing. It drove my father nuts. Everything is broken! But Mom's take was, it's not a scratch, it's a story; it's not a chip, it's character. It was a running joke in our family. "Be careful where you walk, I dropped a cup and there's razor sharp character all over." But it's also true. No one lives a life unscathed. We all have our dents and scratches. It's what makes us, us.

I've always felt that if you're not a little nervous about what you're creating, then what's the point of creating it? When I look back at the work I've done, the projects I'm proudest of are not the ones that get closest to the buffed and polished image of perfection; they are the ones that would have been something else entirely without me because I brought something uniquely my own, some piece of my history—my experiences with depression, loss, failure, success, change.

People polish their cars, shine their shoes, apply concealer. We try to conform to the unblemished model, to hide our scratches and dents. And who can blame us? Leaving those wounds open to the world makes us vulnerable to insult, injury, and more pain. It's a risk for sure. But sometimes it's a risk worth taking. Often, leaning into the things we most want to hide—the pain, the struggles, and the losses—helps us find our most distinct voice. By owning the broken parts that come from living a life, we can turn them from mortifying into material, from experience into expertise. We can make them useful by putting them back out into the world in a helpful way. I think of AA sponsors, social justice activists, Mothers Against Drunk Driving, cancer survivor advocates—people who have taken hold of their negative and flipped it to a positive.

There's a lovely sentiment that pops up everywhere from Rumi to Leonard Cohen: The wound is what lets the light in. We all carry pain. It comes in a rainbow of flavors—embarrassment, regret, failure, and so on. These lows, mixed with our successes and highlights, shape our unique perspective on the world. To only work with the good is to miss out on a huge swath of possible inspiration. And the deeper into the dark you go, the more material you can return with to the light. One ruthless but powerful mantra goes: "If you want to write a good book, write what you don't want others to know about you. If you want to write a great book, write what you don't want to know about yourself."[1]

In Joseph Campbell's description of the hero's journey, he points out that time after time, the hero's weakness, their dents and scratches, is eventually recognized as their greatest strength. It's where the unique answer comes from. The answer that only the hero could ever bring.

Clients often ask me for help around their people's sense of purpose. "They need to remember why we're here, why this is important—why they're important." These are leaders who know that they need to engage their employees beyond the paycheck if they want to get the best out of them. But I also hear about this absence of a sense of purpose from individuals. "I'm not sure what I want to do next," "I go through the day on autopilot," "I live for the weekends."

This chapter is about how making ourselves vulnerable can be a powerful path to finding our greatest strengths. Vulnerability, both professionally and personally, is delicate territory. Delicate, but powerful. Because whether we like it or not, pain can be a compass needle pointing us toward purpose.

PURPOSE AND IDENTITY

If you ask people why they do what they do, you can depend on hearing a roll call of answers: I'm good at it, it's fun, it's easy, I just sort of happened into it, I can make good money, it's what was available. All reasonable answers.

But none are a purpose.

You may have a lovely voice. That does not mean your purpose is to sing. That's a talent. You may be able to charm penguins into buying ice cubes. That does not mean your purpose is to be a salesperson. That's a job. You may need to pay your rent. That does not mean your purpose is to earn. That's a goal.

Purpose lives somewhere deeper. It's an engine that can shape those goals, guide your career, and clarify how to use your talents. Your purpose is not who you think you should be; it's who you can't help being. It's the light that the world would be missing if you didn't bring it.

For many years I let my voice be shut out or shut down. So, now I help people find theirs. I use play and creativity to do it. Curiosity and psychology are some of my building blocks. Art. Senses. Metaphor. Those are all things I have an affinity for. But that's my method, not my purpose. The purpose that draws all those elements together like an irresistible center of gravity is a desire to help people recover from, or avoid, the mistakes that cost me. I'm not alone in that. Purpose often seems most resonant when you're giving people the thing you needed when you were once in their place. Purpose is not defined by the answers you have to offer but by the questions you best understand. How often do we hear the origin story of organizations, books, and movies from creators who say, "I wish I'd had this growing up, so I made it so that kids like me can have bigger wishes."

Some are blessed with that clarity early on. Perhaps you were a stellar soccer player and now you're a stellar coach. You know just what someone needs to hear to push them to be their best. But for many of us, finding purpose takes work. We need time to reflect, clear away everyone else's ideas for us, and really examine where we have the most to give. That's where vulnerability can help.

THE VALUE OF VULNERABILITY

Letting people see the real you—the full you—is difficult and risky.

You worry people will judge you. That makes a lot of sense. People love to make themselves feel better by judging others.

You worry they may not like what they see. That's valid. They may not.

You worry they'll be hurt if they learn how you really feel. That's fair. They may.

You worry they'll abandon you if they see the real you. That's reasonable. People can be unpredictable.

You worry it's too late to change. That's understandable. It's hard to disentangle your core self from your learned behavior.

You worry about what you'll find if you look too closely. That, too, is perfectly valid. There's a reason we bury parts of ourselves, and those reasons don't go away just because you're finally willing to face them.

So why bother with vulnerability? It sounds like a terrible risk. And, yes, many, many, many people would agree and say you should keep your guard up because the risks are too great. What's interesting is how often those very people change their tune once they themselves actually step over to the other side of vulnerability. I've seen a pretty consistent trend: People who have kept their guard up feel they're making the smart or only choice. And yet people who have let their guard down can't imagine going back. They shake their heads at all the time / relationships / choices that were dominated by fear. They regret all the time they spent pretending to be someone else.

Without being vulnerable, you are never fully expressing who you are. You don't have to be vulnerable all the time, but vulnerability and authenticity are intricately linked. As author Ryder Carroll (more on him in a moment) points out, "Vulnerability is incredibly tender because you're getting to the nerves, you're getting to the reality that you inhabit, and the person that you really are."[2]

INTROVERT OUTREACH

One of the classic pieces of advice given to ambitious young people entering the working world is to cultivate a "personal brand" that will sculpt the way they are perceived. My personal brand was creative and critical thinking. I polished it up and hid all the dents and scratches as best I could. I worked extra hours to perfect projects while concealing how much I was struggling.

It wasn't until later in my career, when I presented a retrospective of my most successful projects, that I noticed a difference in how I felt about them. At IDEO I'd worked on projects with global reach, projects that helped people in need, and projects that exceeded expectations. But the work I was proudest of was a smaller project whose inspiration came not from best practices but from my own shortcomings. Not coincidentally, it was also my first foray into designing with safe danger.

As an introvert, I have always loathed conferences. Being expected to introduce myself to everyone in my eyeline, quickly broadcast my worth with an elevator pitch, and then rinse and repeat until cocktail hour was torture for a core part of my being. I preferred meaningful, one-on-one conversations and then quiet recovery. But because I'm a grown-up, I did it anyway. I adapted and learned to show up well in those settings, but it was never natural or fun. So, when I was asked to design a conference booth for a nationwide organization, I was...apprehensive. But the challenge—to position the organization as a meaningful resource for cities seeking better futures for their residents—seemed worth the effort.

Conference booths often rely on giveaways or games, and we spent a few days brainstorming fun ideas along those lines. But at the end of a long week, my team and I went up to the roof for air and drinks and I went on a rant about the shallow nature of conference connections. My team, unbeknownst to any of us, shared my frustration. So we abandoned the expected path and decided to use the three minutes of attention we might have with visitors to exchange something of value beyond business cards. We aimed to create a space where they could share what motivates them, inspires them, and drives them to create change.

Our booth design was grounded in what we thought of as an "introvert outreach" approach, cutting through the small talk to zero in on three key feelings that help you really get to know a person: hope, fear, and pride.

My favorite part of the installation was called "Tip Line," which invited people to share private thoughts in a public way. The centerpiece was a nostalgic pay phone that caught people's attention with its insistent ringing as they passed. When they lifted the receiver, they were met with an invitation: "In front of you is a secret screen. Write something true. Something you'd hesitate to say out loud but believe in nonetheless. Your unrealistic hopes for your city. Your silent fears about your community. The tip everyone should know but no one will admit."

Faces went from puzzled to delighted. They slid aside a small door at the base of the pay phone to reveal a touchscreen where they could write their thoughts. No one hesitated.

The secrets they shared ranged from the personal ("I'm starved for beauty") to the professional ("My job is all about lying to the right people") to the profound ("We're all dying, minute by minute, so choose to make your time important"). After a brief delay to preserve anonymity, the confessions appeared on nearby screens, displayed against a backdrop of bright colors to amplify the whispered truths.

The response was incredible. Though intended as a one-off experience, our client was inspired to continue using the Tip Line at other conferences and finally installed it in their corporate headquarters.

Our empathy exercise of introvert outreach grounded the project in a set of specific needs that, ironically, allowed the experience to grow into something that left all our visitors—introvert and extrovert alike—smiling broadly and thinking deeply. I have no doubt that my team would have delivered something stellar if they'd been led by someone else. But I also know that the work we delivered was uniquely informed by my experiences, insights, and, frankly, fears. I was comfortable enough with my team to get vulnerable about my struggles, and they were gracious enough not to judge me for it.

There are myriad scales and perspectives by which our efforts will be judged. There's nothing we can do about that but our best. However, for me, this particular project was a turning point. My personal measure of success became a question of how different the project would have been without me. Of course, I was always thrilled when we created something that overdelivered on the results the client was hoping for. But it was when I knew I'd contributed something uniquely earned from my own experience, when I'd used a wound to create something wonderful, that I felt truly proud.

PURPOSE FUELS PRODUCTIVITY

Volumes of research out there show what a difference it makes when people feel their efforts are tied to a meaningful purpose: higher job performance;[3] increased motivation and deeper engagement;[4] higher productivity and better physical health;[5] increased resilience in the face of challenges, stress, and setbacks;[6] longevity and well-being;[7] more ambitious goal setting and more achievement.[8] The research shows that feeling a sense of purpose at work has been tied to lower absenteeism, increased willingness to share ideas, more engaged employees, and better employee–manager relationships.

Executives often share that finding their purpose is the game changer for speeding up their growth and for allowing them to make a more profound impact, both at work and in their personal life. Clark Valberg, the founder and CEO of the groundbreaking tech company InVision, once told me, "I'm convinced that figuring out your purpose and having the guts to live it is hands down the most vital thing you can do to grow as a leader."[9]

I have, however, also encountered plenty of leaders who reasonably point out that, in an office context, you may not feel like it's your job to help people find their purpose. They're right. Helping others find their purpose is not your job. But I'll say that every great leader I've worked with has helped me understand myself better and inspired me to find new ways that I could contribute to the team beyond my job description. And just like the teachers that inspired me and made a difference, I have a pantheon of leaders I seek to emulate. I can also name the ones who did not inspire me in the slightest. I suspect you have your own lists. As do the people who answer to you.

As a leader, if you want people to feel that they have a sense of purpose within your organization, it's a two-part recipe: feeling valued and adding value. Your people must feel heard, appreciated, and cared for, and they must feel like they add to the work in ways that make them feel capable, important, and trusted.[10] This is both the kind thing to do as a person and the productive thing to do as a leader.

MATTERING MATTERS

"When I die, they'll just hand my laptop to someone else. I doubt they'll miss a beat."

This from a woman who had just explained how her goal for the coming year was to somehow carve out a little weekend time from her nonstop work schedule to eat dinner with her family. I was at the Administrative Professionals Conference in Toronto to host a three-hour workshop and deliver a symposium on helping teams bond better. I'd been invited because executive assistants are often the gatekeepers for leadership and the den parents for teams, so they're frequently asked to plan events meant to bridge silos, build trust, and improve communication.

Throughout the conference, as I chatted with attendees and fielded questions, I wasn't surprised to hear how much mental and emotional bandwidth these professionals devote to their jobs. I also wasn't surprised to hear that this devotion is generally taken for granted. What did surprise me was the huge imbalance between those two—between how very deeply admins cared about the people, the work, and the organization and how very little they felt cared for in return.

"They call me twenty-four/seven. Midnight, weekends, vacations. They don't give my life a second thought."

"The only time people interact with me is when they want something."

"I know all about their lives, their kids, their ambitions. They have no idea that I do ballroom dancing."

These were delivered as facts of life, not complaints. No one expected any of this to change. "It's the job," they said with a shrug.

But is it? What I heard really drove home how draining it can be to show up for a team that doesn't show up for you, and as a result how very important it is to build a workplace culture of connection and psychological safety. The half-day arc of fun, playful activities I hosted gave everyone a chance to feel seen without feeling judged, get vulnerable without feeling exposed, and be curious about each other without feeling intrusive. For many of our attendees, it had never occurred to them that these could be qualities of their workplace.

Feeling like an isolated, unappreciated afterthought does not need to be part of any job. This doesn't mean everyone in the office needs to be best friends, braiding each other's hair at lunch and planning tandem bike trips. But it makes a powerful difference for people's well-being, job performance, and employee retention when there's a sense of emotional reciprocity, mutual investment, and care. Feeling like you don't matter is linked to burnout, anxiety, aggression, depression, and sadly, even a higher chance of self-harm and suicide.[11]

People need to know that they're more than just a replaceable cog, that they're more than their résumé, that they're more than the temporary users of a corporate laptop. People need to know that they matter.

The foremost authorities on the subject agree that a sense of mattering is necessary for us to truly flourish personally and professionally.[12] Studies show that when people feel like they have a purpose and really count, they're kinder to themselves, have better relationships, and believe more in their ability to reach their goals. This is more than just feeling like you're contributing to the world. It's deeper. It's knowing your specific contribution would be missed if you weren't there.

We all need to feel that the world would be poorer for our absence. Too few of us do.

"We think of ourselves as one big happy family of expendable, anonymous cogs."

WHO NEEDS A PURPOSE?

There's an argument that seeking purpose is the privilege of a certain economic class. After all, you can't very well follow your bliss if you're struggling to feed your family. Although there is something to that, I've seen that circumstances don't have to dictate your capacity for happiness and purpose. You set your own scale.

For nearly a decade, I worked at a blue-chip financial institution and my commute was almost a parody of itself. Packed subways that disgorged a flood of expressionless commuters who trudged in lock-step up an endless staircase. I'm sure many of us loved what we did, but it sure didn't show. At the top of the stairs was always an emissary from one of the city's free papers robotically trying to hand out copies ("Paper. Paper. Free newspaper.") to equally robotic passersby.

One day as I approached the top, I was jarred out of my resting-commuter face by a warm, joyful voice belting out, "Good morning, y'all! Lovely to see you! You're gonna do great today, I just know it!" There stood a woman handing out papers with a big smile on her face, singing out sweet words, and making eye contact with anyone who wanted it. It was the strangest thing. I was so taken aback that I just kept going—albeit with a smile on my face. She was there the next day and the next and my smile got bigger and bigger. By the end of the week, we were all saying "Good morning!" back to her (to which she always responded, "It surely is!").

One late-start Tuesday, I found myself climbing the stairs alone and found this lovely woman quietly packing up her leftover papers. I introduced myself and said, "I just want to let you know how much I appreciate what you bring to my mornings. What inspires you to show up like this? Do people take more papers when you're kind?"

"I hope so!" she laughed. "But I'm just being me. Life is hard. Your life is hard. My life is hard. But it makes me happy to see other people happy. Y'all are climbing all those stairs and I know how that feels. I live in a walk-up with my three grandbabies. I know how those stairs can get at you. If my words can make it a little easier for folks, that feels pretty good."

Here was this woman, living a very different set of circumstances from the people in front of her, still offering them her best and being uplifted by it.

I am not, in any way, trying to play down the impact of poverty, systemic racism, or any of the myriad other uphill battles that I haven't had to fight myself. I've had different battles, and I try not to compare pain beyond saying that everyone carries more than they wish they had to. I share this story because it taught me something I've held with me ever since, and I wanted to honor the woman who did the teaching. I won't speculate on what she considered to be her own purpose, but certainly on those mornings it was clear that the purpose fueling her was rooted in having felt something that she wanted to spare others from feeling.

Whether you primarily work with your hands or your head, whether you work in the home or in the office, whether you're out in front or back of house, you have a purpose and you deserve to claim it.

SHAME AND SECRECY

There's a powerful obstacle to vulnerability that's worth calling out here: Shame.

Shame can weigh you down whether you're responsible for it or not. In fact, it very often grows inside because of something done by others. Appropriately enough, shame's greatest source of power is also its Achilles' heel: secrecy. Shame festers in the dark. It's the injury that just keeps on giving. And we continue to be harmed exponentially by those painful experiences when we feel we need to hide them. Its nearest cousins, embarrassment and guilt, are plenty cruel, but they lack the quality that makes shame particularly pernicious—you protect it.

Shame and guilt, though connected, are very different emotions.[13] Guilt can actually lead to positive change in people's behavior, but shame closes people down. Shame is always an anchor. You cannot move forward with it. You carry it with you, always wrapped in its cocoon of lies and secrecy, always ready to bring you right back to that past moment and all the pain it entails. Keeping an injury secret doesn't always lead to shame, but shame always feeds on secrecy.

However, shame cannot survive the light. Once you let the secret out, the burden of shame lifts. The pain won't immediately evaporate (if only...), but it is transmuted into embarrassment or guilt—and that step is crucial movement forward. It allows you to turn a corner, shift your focus from the rupture to the repair.

Putting your energy into the repair does not belittle the pain of the injury; it acknowledges that holding on to that pain can keep you locked in a stagnant, unhappy place. All the experts seem to agree that if you want to move forward you have to let go, whether that means forgiving yourself or someone else. Anne Lamott once shared this great line: "Forgiveness means giving up all hope of a better past."[14] I sat with that line during one of the most difficult stretches of my life, when I really struggled with forgiving someone very close to me. And I was really mad at Anne for this line, because it was so true and so inflexible. Ruptures happen. No matter how unjust or unwarranted, we can't make them unhappen—that's out of our control. But the repair? It's the repair that we can control. And that begins with the vulnerability to conquer the shame and acknowledge the damage.

I'm not going to weigh in on what's best for someone else's mental health. I will simply say that I deeply believe that both the rupture and the repair are sources of insight and power that we shouldn't waste.

NUMBER ONE WITH A BULLET

One of my favorite examples of this is Ryder Carroll, a *New York Times* bestselling author and creator of the Bullet Journal. The Bullet Journal is an analog method for organizing your mind to get things done. Yes, there are lots of organizational tools out there, but the Bullet Journal stands apart because it combines mindfulness, intentionality, and productivity. Converts call it "one of the most elegant and effective productivity systems I've ever encountered" and "a manual for freeing and directing our consciousness."

I bring up Carroll in this context of Vulnerability + Purpose because he's become very open about the fact that he didn't develop the Bullet Journal because of a talent for productivity or an ease with organization. Quite the opposite.

"Everyone said I was dumb," Carroll told me. "I got bad grades, so I was dumb. Year after year from when I was a little kid. The teachers knew I wouldn't get it, so they didn't bother with me."

Carroll had ADHD in a time before they knew what ADHD meant or how to address it. So he was written off. But he still had to go to school, take tests, get his homework done. Through years of trial and error, he found ways to help his brain do what was expected of it. Piece by piece, he developed a unique system of note-taking, reminders, prioritization, calendaring, and many other elements of executive function that others took for granted but that he had to supplement to survive first adolescence, then higher ed, and finally the professional world.

Although these DIY tools helped him succeed, in his head they were still a crutch he used to hide shortcomings. He'd grown up being told he was stupid. He never wanted to hear that ever again. Those early experiences shaped the way he looked at himself and the way he assumed the world looked at him. So he hid his damage and his crutches. "I never planned to share any of this. Not in a million years. It was deeply embarrassing."

Obviously, Carroll was not alone in trying to hide what he saw as a liability. Many of us try to hide some part of our lives we fear will cost us in the eyes of others—our bodies, brains, hearts, families, choices, histories, mistakes. Of course we do. People are drawn to confidence and capability. Who wants to surround themselves with people who will disappoint them? So you better hide all those disappointing parts, cover the bags under your eyes, and put your best foot forward. Obviously. But there's an even more insidious level to our fear of judgment: the fear that the criticisms are true, that if we let our guard down, everyone will see us for who we really are. And abandon us.

So, that could have been that. Carroll could have had a lovely career working somewhere impressive doing something well. But then a friend of his started planning her wedding. She had four overflowing notebooks, a mountain of business cards, and everything was covered in Post-it notes and tears. So Carroll said, Hey, you know, I've got something that might, um, could, well, maybe help a little, if you'd like. He spent the next forty-five minutes walking her through his tools in case they might be useful for her planning. Essentially, he showed her how his mind worked.

"When I was done, she was staring at me with her mouth hanging open. I was hit with a wave of fear, like, Oh no. What have I done? She thinks I'm nuts."

But that wasn't what she thought at all. What she thought, and said, was, "You have to share this with people."

"It was the first time in my entire life I had ever considered that this was not just a crutch for my brain," Carroll said. And so he took his friend at her word and wrote down the entire Bullet Journal method in a single, feverish weekend and it became a huge success and here we are.

Just kidding. That's not what happened. One of the cruelest things many of us do to ourselves is assume that, if it's our idea, it's no good. We assume someone else already thought of it. We assume we're missing some obvious flaw. We assume they'll laugh at us. So we keep our thoughts to ourselves. Carroll was relieved and flattered by his friend's praise but was mostly just pleased to have helped a friend. He continued working somewhere impressive doing something well. He continued hiding much of who he was.

It took a full five more years of seeing the impact those bits and pieces of his system had on the lives of others before he finally decided to go public with it.[15]

And over time it caught on. In a big way. International best seller. Chapters of devoted fans opening up in city after city around the world. This time I'm *not* kidding. Carroll had turned his wounds into a weapon. The thing that he thought was holding him back had opened a whole new path for him. What he'd thought was just a way to help survive his own circumstance led him to a way to help others thrive in theirs.

Even if the story ended here, it would be incredibly instructive and inspiring. But something interesting happened when Carroll shared his hard-earned insight with the world: The world shared its insights back. He opened their eyes to possibilities they'd missed; they opened his eyes right back.

People were taking all these tools intended to help organize the world around them, and they were using them to help organize the world inside them. Specific Bullet Journal communities emerged that used the journal in deeply personal ways Carroll hadn't anticipated—to manage PTSD, grief, learning disabilities, and hospice caregiving. "They were using this tool to get vulnerable in a way I personally couldn't imagine. I was shocked at how personal the things they would share would be. But one person's vulnerability made it easy for others to open up. That's what caught me off guard. Somebody would share, 'Today, I got real close to the edge, but I asked for help.' Somebody else in the comments would say, 'Because I read this, I didn't step over the line either. Thanks.'"

Vulnerability and purpose had not been on his radar at all. Carroll had created this incredible organizing tool, and everyone was saying how clever and smart he was to have come up with it. The last thing he wanted to do was prove that wrong. "At that point in my life, I never in a million years would have shown you my personal notebook because it revealed what a mess I was day-to-day," he said. "That's not something I was willing to broadcast to the world. I wasn't leading that charge. I was coming from a place where I was broken. I tried desperately to hide it for most of my life.[16] But when I saw the way that other people were being vulnerable with my work, I felt called to risk sharing more from a personal vantage point. That's when I opened up about my struggles with ADHD and the origins of the method. And that switch really pushed me to a whole new stage of life."

GET VULNERABLE TO CONNECT WITH PEOPLE

When I asked Carroll about what that sort of honesty had cost him, he laughed. "Plenty. And nothing. In some cases, I disappointed people. They liked the person they thought I was. Fine. It's not personal, it's about their appetite. But those people who do care about me, they accept the real me."

If you want to connect with somebody, they need to know who you really are. Because if they do not, they are not really with you. They're with whatever projection, whatever character you're pretending to be. This change presents the people in your life with a new opportunity: to like you, to love you. The real you.

"I reached a point in my life where I'd rather be alone with myself than together with somebody where I'm playing a character," Carroll said. "But I haven't had to be alone. I've been with people who genuinely want to be with the genuine me."

GET VULNERABLE TO CONNECT WITH PURPOSE

My father could be an annoying man. For example, when I explained some decision I'd made by saying, "I didn't have a choice," his inevitable, annoying response was, "You always have a choice." Sure, if by choice you mean losing my job, friend, prestige, place in line. Some choice. But in an equally annoying sense, he's right. We are all creating our own lives day by day, either by pursuing the life that we want to create or accepting the life that is being created for us. If you want to live your own life, you have to choose a life rooted in who you are, not who others imagine you to be.

"Whenever people said, 'be yourself,' I took that to mean be your *best* self," Carroll said. "It never occurred to me that being yourself means to be who you are, all of it, top to bottom. It took a while, but eventually the fear of being trapped in a life that wasn't my own finally outweighed the fear of losing the status quo."

Of course, there's a huge difference between vulnerability in your professional life and vulnerability in personal relationships. But there is a core principle at work that does cut across both landscapes: not being afraid of showing who you are. By no means should you waltz into your boss's office and launch into that time your mother threw your comics into the fire because you...well, never mind. But you *are* more than your résumé, and you walk into work carrying more than your KPIs. You can't imagine the relief and surprise in people's eyes during a workshop when someone shares their struggle to balance deadlines and family, and others nod, sharing similar challenges. Or when a half-formed idea sparks an imaginative cascade instead of judgmental side-eye. Vulnerability dispenses with masks and strips away pretense—and when you lead with it, others are often grateful to follow.

Is this a promise that vulnerability always pays off? Nope. It's simply a promise that the people who have made the trip into this new world have found that it was worth what it cost them. And make no mistake, it can cost. The difference seems to be that in the moment it feels like it's breaking the bank, but in hindsight it looks like Monopoly money. Yes, it's gone. But it only really mattered when you volunteered to play that game. Outside of the game, you're free to focus on things with real value.

ACTIVITY

Homegrown Heroes

Hotel conference rooms can suck the life out of any event. Something about the ubiquitous taupe inspires a look that says, "Well, I'm going to die of boredom, but at least I'm not at work."

One cloudy November day, fifty-two people filed into one of these generic conference rooms. This was a talented group, but they'd never jelled as a team. As of the latest quarterly review, most of them felt disposable and unable to bring their whole selves to work (understandable after two recent rounds of layoffs). This offsite was designed to change that.

They all arrived with that taupe look on their faces, but it was quickly wiped away when they saw the table in the middle of the room spilling over with a rainbow of pom-poms, neon slinkies, sparkling stickers, pipe cleaners, and mini mirrored disco balls. Amid all this stood foot-tall wooden artist's mannequins, starkly bare against the riot of colors. Whatever they had expected, this wasn't it.

The activity would have three main beats: talking, making, sharing.

To begin, I pointed out that, although we've studied and practiced the skills on our résumés, that's not all we bring to the table. There are also unique traits we've developed because of our unique lives—the emotional superpowers we've developed in response to our circumstances.

For example, I have a friend who is great at dealing with difficult people. She's not intimidated by loudness or aggression because she grew up surrounded by difficult people and those circumstances shaped her. Another friend's constant moves as a child made him great at turning strangers into friends because he had to learn to feel at home in new and strange environments. But we all have emotional superpowers of one sort or another, and this activity is about helping people identify and share theirs.

In groups of three I had them each share one of their emotional superpowers and its origin story. Then there was a playful twist: I had them translate their emotional superpowers into comic book superpowers. For example, my friend who is good at dealing with difficult people is very hard to offend. You could say she's got thick skin. So maybe her comic book power is bullet-proof skin or Teflon skin, where everything just slides off like water off a duck.

As I walked around, I overheard a petite woman explain that she was really good at caring for others because she had been responsible for her many siblings while her mother worked evenings. A large man with bulging muscles nodded and quietly offered that he was good at bringing teams together because he, too, had been asked to do more than his share for the family as a child. The two of them looked at each other with a recognition that was clearly new to each.

In another group a woman laughingly admitted that she was excellent at lying and catching lies because she'd been raised by people struggling with alcoholism and had needed to develop those skills early on to get by. The others in the group were fascinated, asking respectful but honest questions. With a wry humor the speaker shared pointers such as, "Arguing with someone drunk is like trying to blow out a light bulb."

Next, each group combined their comic book superpowers into a single superhero (including name, powers, catch-phrase, and costume) and brought it to life as an action figure using one of the little naked mannequins and all those materials that had caught their eye when they arrived. I set them loose to think through the nuances and implications of all those emotional qualities—qualities that quite often were hard earned through challenging times, but in this creative, colorful context became something to celebrate.

I'd imagined capes and a silly emblem, but the groups really let their imaginations fly. There were giant flapping ears, kimonos fashioned out of iridescent paper, a feathered headdress. One group made working roller skates for someone whose superpower was rolling with whatever comes.

Finally, I gathered everyone back together and one by one each small group shared the origin stories of their individual emotional superpowers, how those emotional powers had been translated into comic book superpowers, and how they brought that all to life in the action figure. They showed off bionic limbs, hundred-eyed heroes, mirrored shields, and golden guitars. People in the audience jumped in with thoughtful questions about the origin stories. "How do you manage your depression today?" "Did you ever tell your sister how you felt?" "Why do you think music made such a difference?"

By the end, a number of levels had been at work beneath the surface. There was a level of pretty deep self-reflection as people thought through their own history and behaviors and made new connections or reflections. Then there was the bonding that happened in the small groups as people got vulnerable and had that vulnerability rewarded with kindness and generosity and inevitably heard from others whose own stories had parallels. We may know each other in a professional sense, but oftentimes these more personal qualities can go unspoken or unrecognized. For a lot of people, these traits and especially their origins are not typical topics of workplace conversation. But this activity gave them permission to own their story and publicly celebrate what they bring to the world.[17] Finally, the group share essentially created a catalog of strengths that the team brings to the table as a whole, and everyone could see how their qualities complemented one another's.

There were fifty-two people in that room. That means 1,326 separate relationships[18] that this ninety minutes could infuse with new understanding, new appreciation, new connection. But most importantly, it had the potential to help fifty-two people reflect on the path their unique circumstances had placed them on.

HOMEGROWN HEROES: SUPERPOWERED SELF-REFLECTION

Primary Quality
Trust

Supporting Themes
Connection
Vulnerability
Problem-Solving

The What

Self-assessment can be tricky on both a personal and an organizational level. This activity is a fun way of making that reflection manageable and memorable by turning flaws into features.

The How

Share: We each have a skill set that we've studied and refined over the years. But that's not all we bring to the table. We've all also developed unique traits because of our unique lives, characteristics we've developed in response to our circumstances. Think of these as our emotional superpowers.

In small groups (four people per group is our preferred number because it's intimate enough to afford safety but large enough to bring variety), participants take turns sharing one of their emotional superpowers and its origin story. Then each group translates their emotional superpowers into comic book superpowers.

Create: Each group gets thirty minutes to combine their superpowers into a single superhero and bring their hero to life as an action figure (including name, powers, and costume).

Share Back: One by one, each groups shares the emotional superpowers that each team member contributed and how those emotional powers translated into the superpowers of the hero.

Once every hero has been shared, open the floor for comments, then close out with the why.

The Why

Sharing personal anecdotes of triumph allows people to shine in new ways in the eyes of their colleagues, and owning up to weaknesses creates the vulnerability needed to truly empathize with each other as human beings.

In the small groups, participants can see how the qualities of their teammates complement or compensate for their own—emphasizing the value of teamwork. When all the cohorts are brought back together, this pantheon of powers and vulnerabilities can lead into a discussion about the larger group's best qualities and areas for growth.

The Materials

12-inch mannequins, glue guns, scissors, tape, markers

Imagine a kindergarten art room: pipe cleaners, pom-poms, googly eyes, markers, popsicle sticks, fabrics, felts, mirrors, gem stickers, beads, feathers, string, disposable coffee cups, air-dry clay, balloons, wooden blocks, anything else within reach

AIM FOR A MOVING TARGET

Just as we're (hopefully) continuing to grow year after year, so, too, can our sense of purpose shift and change. Although Carroll continues to offer the Bullet Journal method and materials, his perspective on their value has grown with his experience using and sharing them.

"In my life, the Bullet Journal has had three stages so far. The original was one of productivity. I told myself that if I could become productive, I'd be happy. That wasn't true. I got super productive, did all the things, and felt empty. The next stage was purpose. Why am I doing what I'm doing? And that helped tremendously. Now I find myself beginning a third era, which is presence. How am I showing up for my purpose? How am I showing up at my job? In my relationships? For myself?"

That's a big shift from where he started—trying to hide his struggles. At each stage of this growth there's a give-and-take between safety and danger. What was safe became sterile. What was dangerous became irresistible. Then the pins reset and there's a new standard of safety and danger. That push and pull between the two is what creates the space for us to move comfortably (or otherwise) from one stage of our lives to another.

THE PURPOSE OF VULNERABILITY

One of the moments that can sting most is when we realize that we don't get to choose our purpose. It chooses us.

Because of what they went through in their youth, T'ancháy Redvers, a queer television writer and performer, cofounded We Matter, an organization that aims to teach Indigenous youth about how "systemic and structural forces" make it more difficult to feel valued and shares stories of Indigenous people surmounting those forces.

Eliana's Light is a foundation that supports families with children facing medical complexities. It was founded by the family of little girl who was born with a heart condition called dilated cardiomyopathy, underwent three open-heart surgeries and a heart transplant, but eventually passed away before her fourth birthday. Her family's pain was indescribable. But that pain focused them on a mission to support other families faced with what they went through.

Please remember, you need not endure something tragic to have a clear purpose. I offer these as examples of experiences that could have broken people but that instead led to a new path. We all carry echoes of our own particular challenges. When sifting through our interests to get to a sense of purpose, we naturally look at the world and decide how we want to add to it. But what stands out to us as worthwhile is more than a matter of taste—it's an intuition based on what resonates with our history. But you can't feel a resonance unless you're honest. Genuine vulnerability—both to yourself and to others—is about releasing your grip on who you think you should be and taking honest stock of who you are. That means taking the hard look at all you're protecting, all that you're keeping secret, and how you've been doing that. It also means deciding that the armor you once put on to protect yourself is now getting in the way of who you want to be.

One frequent comment I laughingly get from participants is, "I didn't realize I was getting a free therapy session today!" It took me a while to pinpoint why this comment always deflated me. After all, it's meant as a compliment, and given how often our sessions help people connect new dots, recall lost stories, and recognize tired patterns, it's not surprising. The problem is that it implies the only place to open up and talk about your feelings

"Why don't we cuddle anymore?"

is in therapy. But we should be comfortable sharing a bit of our inner lives in a space that doesn't require a co-pay. One of the lovely surprises with vulnerability is how much telling your story to others can help you learn about yourself.

A sense of purpose, however we pinpoint it, has been shown to yield better leaders, better decisions, better sleep, fewer regrets. Our dents shouldn't define us, but they certainly shape us, and being vulnerable enough to understand that shape is what can make all the difference in finding a truly satisfying and meaningful path forward.

HABIT BUILDER

Intentions

One interesting trick I've found around purpose is to slow it down. Instead of trying to lasso your life's purpose in one go, it can help to just look at your day's purpose. For the next week, try setting an intention each morning. This is not a to-do list. It's not about what you're going to accomplish but about why and how you are going to show up in the world today. Less "To rock this shareholder meeting," and more "To broaden people's sense of what's possible."

If you're not sure where to start, a reliable daily option is "What is the world asking me to pay attention to?"

Once you have that clear in your mind, keep returning to it throughout the day and let it animate all that you do.

CHAPTER SIX

TO ENERGIZE BOLD THINKING, INSPIRE CURIOSITY

SHORT-CIRCUIT YOUR SHORTCUTS

Your brain loves shortcuts. Not because it's lazy, but because it's brilliant. The brain seeks out patterns and uses them to build rules to live by: Red strawberries are ripe, smiling people are safe, Beau the barista means a free cookie. These mental shortcuts, shaped by experience and assumptions, speed us through our days.

The catch? Once the brain adopts a habit of thought, it's tough to break. It's comfortable. It's familiar. Why would you change? Hence centuries of efficient farming and centuries of enduring xenophobia.

But if you're hoping to break out of stale habits of thought, if you're looking to find new answers to old questions, it requires putting some distance between yourself and those shortcuts. Whether your efforts will lead to "eureka!" or "you're nuts" is impossible to say ahead of time. But you'll never know unless you risk looking deeply at where your assumptions come from and what opportunities they obscure.

That's where curiosity comes in.

"Have you tried doing the same thing, but harder?"

This chapter explores how to use safe danger to cultivate the kind of curiosity that can blow the doors off your mental habits and supercharge your ability to think beyond expectations.

EXPLORER MIND VERSUS EXPLOITER MIND

Children are disgusting. I feel comfortable saying that since I was one and have two. If, by some oddly misplaced sense of protective compassion, you're inclined to disagree, I invite you to ride the NYC subway at three in the afternoon when kids return home from school. You will never doubt again. I'm not talking about runny noses, pizza-sauce fingers, or any combination thereof (although, yes, gross). I'm talking about the way they interact with their environment. I literally cannot count the number of times I've heard a horrified adult wail, "Don't lick that!" I had to hold both of my daughter's hands when we walked through the station because she would drag her fingers along the grimy tiles, the drippy stanchions, the sweaty seats. Yes, children are disgusting. But they're disgusting for a reason: They're explorers.

To go from understanding zilch to understanding enough to survive, evolution wired children's brains to absorb as much information from as many places and senses as quickly as possible—salmonella be damned. Adult brains, however, having acquired the knowledge required to survive, shift from exploring to exploiting. Adults are wired to make the best use of the knowledge they have. The goal, the methods, the priorities are dramatically different between child and adult brains. That's why a toddler wants to stop and inspect every leaf, and you just want to get down the block. The aperture through which kids take in the world is wide open. Everything is equally fascinating. The adult aperture is focused and narrow—don't jump in the puddle to see how big a splash you can make; step over it and get to school on time.

Each mindset has developed to maximize survival during a specific stage in life. But presuming your adult life is not under constant threat, most people could benefit from a bit more of a mix between the explore and the expert minds.

Interestingly, the octopus seems to be the creature most likely to agree with that. An octopus effectively has two different brains—not just a left and a right with different strengths, like ours, but rather a central survival-focused expert brain and completely separate explorer brain matter running throughout its limbs, which are in a perpetual state of discovery. Octopuses have one up on human children in that they both taste and touch with the same limbs—no separate tongue to slow them down—and their tentacles are in constant motion, running over everything within reach.

An adult already knows the subway pole is gross. No need for a taste test. Our exploit mind prefers to stick with what works, honing it, improving it, mastering it. Exploring something risks wasting time, effort, money. Exploring more means failing more. So we gravitate toward being experts rather than explorers.

So we miss out. We miss out on chances to try unfamiliar ideas, to discover unexpected treasures, to show up in unorthodox ways. We miss out on the chance to rethink who we are, what we value, how we spend our time. We miss out on the invitation to know more about ourselves.

If we want to find our own unique voice in the world, we need to find the courage to risk the failure, waste, and distraction that makes the exploit mind bristle. Balancing the explore and exploit mindsets can frame the unknown as something to be enjoyed instead of feared and open us to new experiences, knowledge, and understanding. Explore more so you fail more so you learn more.

So you become more of an expert than ever.

CARING ABOUT CURIOSITY

Why doesn't the sun bump into the moon? Kids are question machines. Is water wet, or does it just make other things wet? Most adults laugh at their questions. Why don't we make our clothes out of food so we always have snacks available? We may patiently answer the question, but we don't take them seriously.

Not because we know all the answers. Because we stop thinking of questions.

Some stop asking questions because they don't see the point. For example, I overheard the following exchange in the café where I'm currently writing this:

> "They discovered that there might be a second dimension of time. Like, what would that even mean? We experience time moving forward and imagine it moving backward, but what would it mean for time to move side to side or up and down instead of only forward and back?"
>
> "Unless that's going to impact the tip jar, please just wipe down the tables so we can go home."

We have enough answers to get through our days and so we assume that if we don't already have an answer, it's not a question worth asking.

For others, it's not that we choose not to ask the questions—it's that we don't even see that there are questions to be asked. Life becomes so familiar, the shortcuts in our brain so engrained, that our mind glides over life's mysteries without pausing to wonder. But those questions are still out there in the shadows.

Curiosity is not just asking the questions; it's recognizing that there are questions to ask. That's the key. Walk down the street and ask yourself how much you understand of what you see. Why don't we see sleeping squirrels? Is it windier in the middle of the street or on the sides near the buildings? Why is your middle finger the longest? Does running in the rain get you wetter?

If civilization collapsed, would you know how to make an umbrella? A tire? Bronze? An arrowhead? A pencil? So much of what surrounds us in life took hundreds of thousands of people, years, and knowledge to end up cluttering our kitchen drawers. And we never give it a second thought. An essay called "I, Pencil: My Family Tree as Told to Leonard E. Read" revels in how much you didn't know goes into making a simple pencil ("Cedar from Oregon, graphite from Sri Lanka mixed with clay from Mississippi that is treated with Candelilla wax from Mexico and covered with 6 coats of yellow lacquer made from castor beans").[1] In 2009, a UK graduate student named Thomas Waites decided to try to replicate a £5 toaster himself. From scratch. Waites focused on just five of the hundred actual ingredients (iron, copper, plastic, nickel, and mica), but it still required visiting old mines in the Forest of Dean, England, the Knoydart Peninsula in Scotland, and the Isle of Anglesey in Wales, learning to smelt iron ore, and making his own plastic from potatoes. In the end his toaster was a glorious, horrifying £1,187 mess.

"And they lived happily ever after, as long as they never dared to question the paradigm again."

The world is spilling over with answers to questions we don't think to ask. Why are they called Oreos? Why didn't we evolve a set of eyes in the back of our head too? Are fish just flying underwater? Why is hair lovely to touch until it falls out and then becomes gross?

If you're looking to encourage bold thinking, in yourself, in your team, in your family, you need to nurture an interest in finding the questions that are not being asked as much as you value finding the answers.

WHY IS CURIOSITY WORTH YOUR TIME?

New ideas don't come from people who have the answers. Innovation comes from the people with the questions. Of course, there's a tax to that: time. It takes time to open questions rather than shut them down. But it can make all the difference. Here's one of my favorite examples.

I know why I skipped class as a kid. So I can guess at why the kids at a rough school in a rough part of St. Louis were skipping school. But I really shouldn't just guess. Luckily, their new principal didn't. She got curious. She took the time to go out into her community and talk to the kids and to the families. She'd been warned to expect apathy and hostility, but she hadn't expected laundry. Again and again, she heard that laundry was a problem—from no access to washing machines to power being cut off even if families had them. Kids were self-conscious about how they looked and smelled. Her district didn't have a budget for books, much less wash-and-fold service, so she got curious about who else could help. She reached out to Whirlpool to see if the company was willing to donate some machines to the school. It was. But not only that, her request sparked curiosity at Whirlpool, which found the same issue in hundreds of schools and started a washer and dryer donation program for schools in need. After one year, 93 percent of students who utilized the donated washers and dryers reported improved attendance.[2]

Curiosity can lead to surprising insights. This is not to say that everyone knows what they need or why they do what they do—but by getting curious you can at least cultivate a richer understanding of the world you want to impact.

QUESTIONING THE OBVIOUS

What does curiosity have to do with safe danger? Everything. Curiosity is both the key to deploying safe danger effectively and one of the traits it helps develop. It's both safe—by putting yourself in the role of explorer rather than expert, you're there to learn, so your ego has nothing to lose—and dangerous, because asking important questions may reveal uncomfortable truths.

When coming up with new activities, I've been inspired by how the brain works, sensory experiences, and creative outlets from mandalas to holograms. But to take an activity from amusing to impactful requires a more deliberate flavor of curiosity.

Clients often voice their frustration that the same voices always fill the room. They usually assume that quiet people are quiet because the loud people are loud. To rectify this, they've tried calling on quiet people, organizing meetings just for quiet people, and even deploying talking sticks.

Taking a curious approach is different. Rather than focusing on solutions, it means backing up and getting curious about the problem first. In this case, I'd want to understand what's appealing about being quiet in such a culture. I'd question the hierarchy of sources and symptoms: Are quiet people excluded because they're quiet or are they quiet because they feel excluded? Are they afraid to fail because they've failed before or because they haven't? I'd get curious about all the variations of danger that hold people back: fear of being laughed at, fear of not living up to expectations, a culture of speaking to top the previous speaker, an assumption that the louder ones are right, an assumption that their opinions are not valuable, a reluctance to call attention to themselves, not enough engagement to bother contributing, the feeling that no one listens to them anyway.

From there, I'd get curious about safety: Is it more comfortable to fail when all together or in private? Does pairing failure with quick success balance it out (like a sour gummy worm)? Do reactions from authority help or hinder?

Using curiosity as a prism to split the situation into more discrete colors allows you to see specific points to address—either as elements to shore up with safety, or as elements you can defang with a little danger—to spark change.

CURIOUS HERO

When researching this book, I naturally wanted to speak to expert practitioners of the qualities in question—the superheroes I admire and continue to learn from. For curiosity, it was a no-brainer: My curiosity superhero is Jad Abumrad, creator of the iconic podcast *Radiolab* and recipient of the MacArthur Genius Grant. Abumrad has built a career on asking fascinating questions (Can a machine be moral? Do plants have memories?), interviewing notable figures (Dolly Parton, Neil deGrasse Tyson, Yo-Yo Ma), and sharing surprising information (bumblebees can play soccer).

My only hesitation in speaking with him was, as someone for whom curiosity obviously comes naturally, would he have any practical advice to offer?

The first words out of his mouth: "I'm not a naturally curious person."

Huh. Okay. Lesson one: Even Batman has to do push-ups.

"Growing up, I always felt shy and awkward. The way a shy and awkward person operates is you walk into a room and you just watch very carefully to see what the world is doing, and then you mimic them. The consequence of that is you end up suppressing the questions that naturally occur. Why are they doing it that way? Why was I doing it this way? You have these questions, but you don't feel permission to ask them."[3]

I find this insight particularly illuminating because, though not everyone may rely so fiercely on deliberate observation to survive social situations, we are all compelled at a cultural, social, and neurological level to behave like the people around us. When in Rome. (The school I went to had a strict dress code, but occasionally, we could earn a "free dress" day. It required hours of effort to earn, but it was all worth it for that glorious Friday when we were able to break free of uniformity and wear outfits that boldly announced our unique identities. Everyone wore jeans and a T-shirt.)

So, if we don't naturally show up the way others do, how to get over that? There are a few familiar paths for handling insecurity:

Don't: We remain shy. We keep our thoughts to ourselves or save them for the trusted few.

Pretend: We fake it. We discover that mimicking is enough.

Enforce: We become cynics or bullies. We insist we're right and anyone different is laughable.

Others, like Abumrad, discover tools that spotlight their distinct value. In his case, it was a microphone. "When I became a journalist, having the microphone and the job description gave me the permission to ask all these questions I just never felt I could ask. It felt like a magic trick."

SAY MORE ABOUT THAT

Over the course of his career, Abumrad came to an interesting realization: Curiosity starts before the question itself. So, he has cultivated a sensitivity to his own dissatisfaction. "The thing that has grown very loud for me is the itch in my brain that says I'm not done. It's like the Princess and Pea—you just know that something is off. You may not know what or why, it may be ten mattresses down, but you know that there's *something* more to look for."

He's learned that knowing exactly what question to ask next is less important than just sensing that there is another question to be asked. "Sometimes when the question isn't there but the itch is, I'll just ask, 'Can you say more about that thing you just said?' People are always happy to elaborate and that's usually enough. It brings me more ideas to swim in until I find the next current to follow."

This reminds me of a technique hostage negotiator Chris Voss speaks about using when he wants people to keep talking: repeating the last three words someone says. They say, "I want the money so that I can get back to nature." So you say, "Back to nature?" And they elaborate, moving from the what to the why, and you discover, "Yeah, I want to get back to nature because my wife left me, but we first met while camping, so maybe a cabin in the woods will bring her back."[4] The *why* reveals what's really going on. The point here is that you don't need to be Jad or Oprah to get curious.

ERUPTION OF DISRUPTION

There was a point in the life of *Radiolab*, Abumrad's flagship show, when the level of work was unrelenting and the joy had slipped away. "Every day felt like climbing a mountain. I'd go to my office, shut the door, listen and listen and listen and cut, cut, cut." He became so focused that he confined his time outside to one square block. Two lefts to pick up coffee, two lefts back to work. He never wandered. He was in such a deep rut that when people wanted some of his time he just invited them to come with him on his loop around the block.

One day, midloop with a friend, he was about to make the last left to go back when his friend suggested they go another block. "I was like, 'Uh, no, I go *this* way.'" But she insisted and dragged him out of his safe loop. On the next block, they came across an odd-looking store called the Compleat Sculptor. "She raised her eyebrows and asked, 'Do you wanna go in?' I said, 'No. No, I don't, I wanna go back and do more work.' But she wasn't having it."

Inside, they discovered a massive art supply shop straight out of a Victorian Steampunk fever dream—skull replicas, iron chisels, creepy stone figures hanging from the ceiling like petrified angels, bins of mysterious brass implements, a wall of silicone textures. "In the basement they were selling boulders—actual boulders." At one point, he sat in a corner reading a trade magazine about fake blood viscosity. "I was like, 'What???' There's so many kinds of fake blood!" They stayed for an hour and a half.

"But here's the thing that stays with me," Abumrad said. "We walked out in a kind of dream state, and at the edge of the sidewalk, I looked down at a manhole cover and my brain just went in a thousand directions. First, it was just a deep appreciation for the miracle of indoor plumbing. I looked around with imaginary X-ray vision at all the pipes under the street that bring us life and pasta water and take away our dirt and waste. I remember being absolutely stunned that we never think about what miracles these really are. I looked up at the sun and had a moment of, *Wow, that is an actual star.* I was overwhelmed by the variety, complexity, and mystery of the world and I suddenly was just…grateful. Grateful for all these unsung miracles. My tunnel vision cracked open and the world poured in."

Remember as a kid when you said a word over and over until it lost all meaning? *Cucumber, cucumber, cucumber.* Abumrad's experience was the opposite—it flooded the world with meaning. "I went back to work with a renewed sense of purpose. All the storytelling became about re-creating that 'manhole on the street' moment."

Abumrad's detour resonated with me because we all need a shake-up sometimes—a surprise to rattle our routines and remind us what we're taking for granted, but one not so jarring that we shut down. A little danger, a little unexpected disruption can be an incredibly powerful way to reignite curiosity and excitement.

"I had walked that loop twice a day for I don't know how long. Twenty steps from the inspiration I desperately needed."

SURPRISE PIVOT

Between the explore and exploit mindsets, I've focused on the former for most of this chapter. That's not because it's more important but because the exploit mindset doesn't need an advocate. It's so ubiquitous we don't even notice it envelops most of the adult world. But to be clear, my experience is that neither is more important; it's the combination that makes them powerful. Like scissors, Reese's, or dynamite, it's so effective because of how the two parts work together. Without the exploit, you can explore until the cows come home, but you'll end up with a treasure chest of potential that lies fallow as the cows stare back. The exploit without the explore is a rerun of stale ideas.

This, of course, begs the question—how to use them together? How to balance the open aperture of the explorer with the tunnel vision of the exploit? What would help is a way to know when your train of thought should switch tracks from one to the other. It turns out there is such a signal: surprise.

SOMATIC SURPRISE

"It's just such a core belief to me that when you tell a story, it should surprise you," Abumrad said. "It should lead you to a revelation you didn't expect."

There's a subtle distinction there that's worth calling out. It's not something you didn't *know*—it's something you didn't *expect*. Absorbing something you didn't know is learning. That's plenty important. But it's not the same as what happens with something you didn't expect. The not-expecting is a key piece of curiosity. Surprise is that X factor.

"When you are surprised, you suddenly are open, it's like a window opens up that shows you the world in an unexpected way," he said. "But if you just tell me what I already know, the window actually closes a little bit. Without surprise, we get even more attached to the way we already think."

The expert mind grows by answering questions. The explore mind thrives by discovering questions it hadn't realized were there.

But that awareness takes practice.

"I should tell you that the staff hated this. Hated it. But it was an important piece of the process," Abumrad said. The *Radiolab* team would have weekly meetings to listen to raw tapes and think through the structure of the story they wanted to tell. It could sometimes be a slog, but this in itself wasn't what Abumrad was talking about. What they hated was when, every so often, there was an interaction or a statement that stood out as special to him, and Abumrad would stop the tape and have everyone close their eyes. He would ask his team, "Okay, where do you feel that in your body? Do you feel it deep in your chest? At the tip of your forehead? Did you lean in or back? What's going on with your breath?" The formal name for this is somatic listening—paying attention to how your body responds to information.

"Everybody has a different experience of what interestingness feels like. If you pay attention, you can sense where it happens in your body," Abumrad said. "Before you know the question, before you even know you have one, the body reacts. It's like a reflex. Your body gives you a signal, and you either learn to hear it or not."[5]

Before we can trust our intuitions, we need to feel them. Hence the pausing of tapes during the staff meeting. Abumrad was particularly sensitive to cultivating this intuition in newer members of his team. He often found that less-experienced creators struggled to find the spark in the story.

"They'd choose the most expected, boring quotes from the interview. So I'd ask, 'Why didn't you use that other part where they're being wonderfully insane? Why didn't you go there?' And they'd shrug and say, 'I didn't feel like I should' or 'I thought the other was what you wanted.' Those are the times when I would say, 'Okay, let's take a step back and tune in to our own sense of surprise. That's our guide.'"

We feel surprise because (1) we had a sense of balance and (2) something knocked us off it. That moment of surprise gives you two big arenas to interrogate. You can get curious about the balance you had—where it came from, why you trusted it, why it wasn't as solid as you expected, what was lost when you lost it. And you can get curious about what caught you off guard—why didn't you see it coming, what possibilities does this open up, what other types of things might this disrupt?

The feeling of surprise before we formulate the questions and answers is not typically something most of us single out and think about. But if you're looking to grow your curiosity, learn to pay attention to surprise and understand it as a signpost to unexpected places for you and your audience—whomever they may be. That's a powerful tool to have at your disposal.

GO NUTS

The magic of getting curious is that you never know what you're going to learn. On a project to improve emergency room safety procedures, a team got curious about not the world's best hospitals, as one might expect, but a NASCAR pit crew. Why? Because familiar environments can blind us to opportunities. So sometimes finding analogous situations with shared qualities can help you approach your own issues with fresh eyes. In this case, both ERs and pit crews require high-pressure nonverbal communication, high levels of precise preparation, and efficient coordination. By switching environments, the research team was able to see blind spots in the surgical workflows that were only obvious with a different context.

The downside of curiosity is that you can't tell ahead of time if it's going to pay off. Exploration is not a guarantee of discovery. Not every treasure map leads to a pirate chest.

On a project to encourage people to stop hoarding their credit card points and to use them more often (hence reaping the benefits from the card and building brand loyalty), we had a brilliant stroke of inspiration and reached out to a world-class expert on squirrels. His specialty was hoarding behaviors.

We were very proud of ourselves for making this connection and spoke to him for two hours. A team member even called in from vacation in Greece. We explored and explored and explored. We found out some fascinating things (squirrels will dig and fill up empty holes using sleight of hand [paw?] to fool other squirrels who may be spying on them). And all that resulted in exactly zero practical inspiration. If there was a practical "there" there, we couldn't find it.

So, no, getting curious doesn't always work. But I do believe it's always worth it. Mostly because it keeps you open to other rays of inspiration, but also because curiosity can be contagious. Although the squirrel expert didn't work for us, that conversation had an amazing ripple effect throughout our community that inspired other teams and elevated the work across our studio. Almost two years later I had a team come show off a brilliant seating concept they'd developed for a major airport after our squirrel research inspired them to look at how millipede legs work.

ACTIVITY

Mash-Up Mindset

Out-of-the-box thinkers excel at connecting disparate ideas in unexpected ways, and—surprise—it's curiosity that spurs them to tinker with seemingly unrelated concepts, disciplines, or experiences. One of my activities to play with these skills, Mash-up Mindset, is, admittedly, a little on the nose.

We started with a box. Big and heavy and closed. People shook it and shoved it trying to interpret the rattles and clunks from inside. Dozens of colored strings stuck out through a flap.

I told everyone to pick one and pull. Out tumbled the objects on the other end of their strings: glow stick, rainbow feather duster, bright orange masking tape, face cream, colored sand, foam earplugs, cocktail shaker, a plastic plant, gardening gloves, ping-pong paddles, a label maker, a set of prisms, a coffee mug, and more.

The talented designer Loren Blackman introduced me to the Japanese term *chindogu*—"weird tool"—which refers to ridiculous combinations of everyday needs and objects to make something delightfully odd. An all-over plastic bathing suit for when you want to go swimming but don't want to get wet or a baby onesie made of mop material so that the little dear can clean the floor while crawling around. Inspired by this, we paired everyone up and gave them twenty-five minutes to somehow combine the objects they'd received and invent a chindogu of their own.

Ideas flew fast and wild—terrible ones mostly, but in this case those were the most fun. Plus, that process of generating and generating and generating reveals how deep and rich your thinking can go when you let it off its leash. It fuels the optimistic curiosity that comes from starting at zero and crafting something into existence that (no matter how silly, ridiculous, or brilliant) is uniquely yours.

Some teams combined intended uses, like pairing feather duster with cocktail shaker to reward yourself during spring cleaning. Others focused on form over function, reimagining ping-pong paddles and sand-filled balloons as self-balancing hors d'oeuvre plates.

Share backs were faux infomercials, hilariously framing the creations as life-changing inventions. *Tired of wasting hours moisturizing your hands after planting tulip bulbs? Never again! Now your green thumb can always be soft and supple thanks to Marvelous Moisturizing Garden Gloves* (gloves filled with face cream). *Too shy to shoot the breeze with your colleagues? Never fear, the bottom of the "Coffee Chandelier" mug is equipped with dangling prisms that make it impossible to set down, so you have no choice but to walk around chatting!*

It was fun and silly, but the goal was deeper: to practice stripping away the obvious, rewinding from answers back to questions, uncovering overlooked potential.

MASH-UP MINDSET: COLLISIONS OF INNOVATION

Primary Quality
Collaboration

Supporting Themes
Problem-Solving
Creative Thinking
Storytelling

The What

Invent ridiculous combinations of everyday needs and objects to make something delightfully odd.

The How

Surprise: Pair people randomly. Then have everyone gather around a large, closed box with a variety of colored strings sticking out, take a string, and on the count of three, pull. When the box opens, everyone finds some odd object at the end of their string.

Create: Each pair gets twenty-five minutes to invent a mash-up from their two objects, including a name, tagline, and value proposition for their creation.

Share: Share back is in the form of an infomercial for the product, with a before and after segment. When every item has been advertised, close with the why.

The Why

This activity inevitably starts with a round of brainstorming—ideas flying fast and furious. Terrible ideas mostly (although, in this case, the worst ideas are often the most fun). But that process of generating and generating and generating is powerful. It shows how deep and rich your thinking can go when you let it off its leash. It's an opportunity to start from zero and together craft into existence something that is (no matter how silly, ridiculous, or brilliant) uniquely yours.

The Materials

Collection of random stuff—I went to a thrift store and grabbed whatever tickled my fancy (glow sticks, rainbow feather dusters, rolls of brightly colored masking tape, face cream, colored sand, foam earplugs, cocktail shakers, plastic plants, gardening gloves, ping-pong paddles, a label maker, prisms, coffee mugs)

Glue guns, duct tape, scissors, string

CURIOUSER AND CURIOUSER

People often conflate *new* ideas with *innovative* ideas. They're not the same. Boldly innovative ideas are fueled by more than novelty. A truly innovative idea so displaces an accepted, obvious way of doing things that it becomes the only way you can imagine doing things. Sometimes it's something that you paradoxically recognize as familiar the first time you see it ("Of course my phone should be my camera too"); sometimes it takes time to muscle the old out of the way ("A horseless carriage? Yer nuts."). But, either way, innovation is the invention of a new "obvious."

Our expectations form a barrier to new thoughts, so to get there, we first have to distance ourselves from the old "obvious." Start by getting out of your echo chamber and giving yourself permission to have been wrong all along. Practice being guided by your own moments of surprise. Make being an explorer as important as becoming an expert.

REDISCOVER DISCOVERY

If you want to deliver unexpected solutions, start by asking unexpected questions. That's easier for some than for others. There's a moment (or many moments) when we may recognize we've lost that curious part of ourselves, realize how much that loss has cost us, but not know how to get back to it. We remember being curious once upon a time, but—like a language studied in high school—the vocabulary has slipped away. This might be you—or your entire team.

Activities like Chroma Aroma (see page 206), Delightful Doppelgängers (see page 210), Mash-up Mindset (see page 114), and Memory Floss (see page 237) use safe danger to create small opportunities to jump the tracks of thought, to question the obvious, to turn the accepted inside out. They force you to abandon the mental shortcuts your brain relies on and take the long way around to places you didn't know you were looking for.

Cultivating curiosity starts with trusting our intuition about what's worth exploring—and then actually exploring it. The next chapters zero in on the qualities of optimism, connection, and trust, which I've seen make that exploration possible.

HABIT BUILDER

Re-Create the World

"When I walk down the street," Abumrad said, "I sometimes play a game and ask myself how much of what I see could I re-create. Not just the snazzy things like smartphones or planes but also simpler ones—a billboard? A window? A sidewalk? How do you create concrete from scratch? Smooth it out? Calculate seasonal expansion so it doesn't crack?"

This is an excellent way to flex your curiosity muscles. If you're feeling bold, you might even share your questions with others—you'll feed your curiosity, lower your embarrassment threshold, and discover all the weird stuff the people around you actually know.

An easy build on Abumrad's idea is to carry a small notebook for jotting down questions, sudden insights, or gems you overhear. (On a crowded subway I once heard a very elderly lady telling her friend, "So I says to him, I says, 'Get that fish out of your ear.' And you know what? They went to the finals that year. So there you go!" Without my notebook, that glorious exchange might have been lost to the ages.)

Keep it even simpler. For a week, try a new route each day. Get off one exit earlier or later, take a side street. Go the long way around. Explore.

CHAPTER SEVEN

TO FOSTER RESILIENCE, INSPIRE OPTIMISM

"FALL DOWN SEVEN TIMES, GET UP EIGHT." "A SMOOTH SEA NEVER MADE A SKILLED SAILOR." "When the going gets tough, the tough get going." Resilience in the face of defeat is one of the most powerful qualities a person can bring to the table. In a professional setting, it fuels problem-solving, flexibility, and long-term success by helping navigate uncertainties, insane deadlines, awful colleagues, or soul-crushing missteps without losing focus or motivation. On a personal level, resilience helps you manage relationship disasters or painful loss with emotional balance and perspective. All this is key to mental well-being and sustained success across all areas of life. No wonder corporations, teams, parents, and schools want to foster resilience.

Resilience is often attributed to stubborn determination, but that's to sell it short. Resilience isn't about refusing to accept the situation; it's about believing in yourself—in your capacity to overcome setbacks. And that belief is fed not by stubbornness or denial but by optimism.

AN ATTITUDE OF ALTITUDE

Optimism gets a bad rap. It's pigeonholed as a light and fluffy thing about glasses of water. It's often dismissed as a naive veneer of cheerfulness covering a failure to understand the gravity of a situation. ("It's actually wonderful that we blew a tire way out here! Now we can spend quality time together without the distractions of food, water, or civilization!") But at its best, true optimism is actually a steely, powerful thing.

A look at the current research makes a pretty strong case for encouraging it:

- Optimists tend to earn more, have better job security, and are more likely to be promoted.[1]
- Optimists are more likely to make smart financial moves, and optimistic salespeople outsell pessimists by 56 percent.[2]
- Optimists also tend to make better leaders.[3]

Should you stubbornly refuse to acknowledge when things go sideways? Nope. That sort of behavior drives reasonable people out of their minds and into the clutches of pessimism. Pessimists see themselves as the ones facing reality. However, they are also likely to see themselves as helpless to do anything about it and give up before the fight begins. Pessimism serves many purposes that we'll get to later, but building persistence and resilience is not part of that agenda.

Real optimism isn't blind faith in success or smiling through the pain. Real optimism is about seeing reality clearly—warts and all—and still believing that success, though difficult, is possible. It's a solution-focused mindset committed to action and earned by going through enough dark tunnels to know light will come if you keep moving forward. Crucially, it's also the

"I now pronounce you fifty percent likely to file for divorce in less than eight years."

ability to emerge, be disappointed, and still seek the next tunnel. You have to risk being disappointed. But what makes that risk worth taking is that it builds the resilience you need to face disappointment without being defeated by it. Optimism isn't naive confidence that your journey will be a success; it is justified belief that the journey—wherever it leads—will be valuable.

So, what makes a journey valuable? Well, obviously, when it's a success. And success encourages future optimism. So that's a lovely, self-reinforcing loop. But also a short-sighted one. No business, no leader, no athlete, no artist, no musician, no investor, no parent, no child, no creature with a pulse has an unbroken line of unqualified successes. But a failed journey can be incredibly valuable if you know how to use it. So, yes, success is one way to make the journey worth the effort. But it isn't the only way.

THE WORD *FAILURE*

One way to build up the optimism for resilience is by defanging failure.

People have various—often visceral—reactions when I use the word *failure*. Most want to soften, replace, or dodge it altogether. "Can we use the word *misstep*? *Setback*? *Learning opportunity*?" Sure you can. But I don't. If replacing the word *failure* with something less charged makes a conversation easier, then that's fine for a quarterly review or parent–teacher conference, where you need to be diplomatic and encouraging. But it also allows the source of that discomfort to stay firmly lodged in place. The fear, hopelessness, blame, and humiliation that are wrapped up in the word *failure*—all those things get to keep their seats in the mind and heart. But, in our case, the point is to address the source of that discomfort, not avoid it.

The word *failure* makes people uncomfortable. That's why I use it.

PLAYING WITH FAILURE

When my daughter was five, she watched with envy as the bigger kids at the playground sped hand over hand across the rings. Whenever it was her turn, she froze. It was a long way down for a three-foot human. So, I led her to the middle, lifted her up, and made sure she had a good, secure grip. Then I told her to let go. I told her to fall. There was a back-and-forth of panic, reassurance, hesitance, and finally trust. She dropped, crumpled, and bounced back up.

"That's as bad as it gets, Honey," I told her. "Worst case. That's it."

She never hesitated at the rings again because she knew (1) what failure felt like, and (2) she could survive it.

Consider inviting more failure into your life. Not out of masochism but to develop a practice of courage. As any fan of Nelson Mandela (or Harry Potter) knows, "Courage is not the absence of fear but rather the triumph over it."[4] Fear of failure holds almost everyone back. But the more chances you give yourself to fail, the more you'll know (1) what it feels like, and (2) that you'll survive it.

FAILURE TO PRACTICE

The stories we tell ourselves through art, myths, and fairy tales often show that the road to growth runs through danger. Very rarely do we tell the story of a hero who sets out and immediately falls off a cliff, the end. In the stories we tell, persistence is rewarded. But let's face it, the nature of risk is that success isn't guaranteed; it's not an equation: Effort = Success. Exploration means risking coming home empty-handed. If you get home at all. Businesses fail, art goes unbought, athletes go home without a medal. No wonder we sigh with relief when the danger passes. Even in the stories that spur us toward courage, once the third-act danger has been vanquished, the music swells and the credits roll. They basically say: "Glad that's over! Let's get comfy again forever after."

Generally speaking, if you want to be less intimidated by failure, there aren't a lot of shortcuts. It's mostly a Nike-esque situation: Just do it, or don't. But, in this case, I've got something for you that actually makes it easier to brave the threat of failure: practice.

Pros don't show up on game day without training. In fact, they spend *more* time practicing than playing, getting it wrong until they get it right, building muscle memory so that the moves are second nature when it's time to perform. Practicing failure with safe danger activities has the same benefits.

Growth means facing danger. There is always going to be uncertainty, risk, and vulnerability. But none of those require fear. Danger, yes. Fear, no. Fear may crash the party, but it need not be the guest of honor. If we can take the sting out of failure, turn it to our advantage, make it a tool, then we don't have to fear it. By practicing failure safely, you can shift it from an enemy to be feared to an ally to be valued and build the emotional muscle memory that makes resilience second nature.

FROM HEARING TO HABITS

IDEO's culture valued taking risks and quickly learning from failures, but we couldn't afford to fail completely—we had clients to please, tight deadlines, and we all wanted to make a difference. So, we aimed to take only the risks worth taking. Yet failure still happened—and it still hurt. There's a beautiful scene in the film *Lawrence of Arabia* when a fellow soldier watches Lawrence calmly put out a flaming match with his fingers. The soldier eagerly tries it himself, burns his fingers, and shouts, "Hey! It hurts!"

"Certainly it hurts," Lawrence says.

"What's the trick then?" the exasperated soldier asks, coddling his burned fingers.

"The trick," Lawrence explains, "is not minding that it hurts."

I wanted to find a way for people to practice burning their emotional fingers so that when it happened in real life they weren't distracted by surprise, shock, or pain, but rather in a position to recognize all those feelings, tip their hat in greeting, and move on. Lists of pointers and tips aren't enough; turning hearing into habits is hard (See: healthy eating, more exercise, flossing). Just like my daughter on the rings, talking about failure isn't enough; it needs to be felt.

But what flavor of failure?

- Failing at something you're *not* good at, like a new sport for the very first time?
- Failing at something you *are* good at, like the star athlete striking out?
- Failing because of *outside* forces, like slipping on icy pavement?
- Failing because of *inside* forces, like being too embarrassed to ask for help after slipping?
- Failure when it's *hopeless*, like cooking a strange dish without a recipe?
- Failure when you're *hopeful*, like thinking you've mastered Grandma's cheesecake recipe, only to discover it tastes like cardboard?

So many ways to fail! Each stings in a unique way and can lead to different types of responses, recriminations, rethinking. And how to make the danger safe? I wanted a fun, joyful way to practice failing, one that inoculated people against the fear of it without humiliation or judgment. Failure without consequences.

ACTIVITY

Unblinking Line

The tables filled with three types of people: the *nervous* (why, oh why did I agree to this?), the *hungry* (bring it on), and the *unconvinced* (win me over). In the crowd, I spotted Edward—sharp and thoughtful, but so petrified of not getting work perfect that he took forever, drove his team nuts, and muddled useful efforts in a flood of overkill. His team had dragged him to the session. I hoped he wouldn't regret it.

"You all do hard things, tackle tough challenges, solve deep problems," I said. "So, today's activity is super easy and straightforward."

Expectant eyes.

"And you're going to fail."

Confusion. Disbelief. Laughter.

"You're going to fail badly. No matter how talented or untalented you think you are, this will be a disaster. And that's the point. So just lean into it. The instructions are simple: You have one minute to look into the eyes of the person across from you and draw their portrait."

Chuckles. Confidence from the talented. Panic from the rest.

"But you are *only* going to look into their eyes. You are not allowed to look down at your page. And you're not allowed to lift up your pen. These are the two cardinal rules—no lifting up, no looking down."

Groans from all. Defiance from the determined.

Edward looked...exasperated. Not angry, per se, but annoyed he was wasting time on something silly when he had serious work to do. Would he leave? I never want anyone to feel forced to do something. Obliged to try, fine. But forcing is no way to earn trust. It had to be his choice. He had a look like a waiter just told him the only dessert left was broccoli butterscotch sorbet—but he stayed. I'd take it.

"You have one minute...starting now."

As everyone began to draw, two things immediately happened: laughter and apologies. "Ugh! I think I just gave you two noses and they're both in your ear!" The seconds ticked by, each page filling with more and more squiggles, the room filling with more and more laughter. I also noticed people constantly looking down and lifting their pens.

Before the next round, I tried to articulate why this was more than a silly game.

"Resilience in the face of defeat is one of the most powerful qualities a person can bring to the table. But it's hard to practice. Resilience needs something to bounce back from, and most people don't sign up to get kicked down an emotional staircase. But this is a playful moment of failure for everyone so that, in miniature, you get that feeling of facing defeat and getting up for another try."

Second round, same rules, no looking down, no lifting up applied. But now a new partner and a new wrinkle: "This round is inspired by my daughter. She's a cute kid, but her kindergarten school photos looked like a psycho killer in a wind tunnel. Eyes were bulging, neck strained, smile straining from ear to ear. Like this." I demonstrated, abandoning all pretense of dignity. "It turned out that she was smiling from the inside out—based on how she thought a big smile should feel. She wasn't just smiling with her lips, she was smiling with her teeth, her nose, her earlobes." I paused. "And for our next round that's what I'm going to ask of you. For sixty seconds, I'd like you to smile like a psychotic kindergartner."

Groans and laughter. Another minute of joyful failing, of Picassos and Modiglianis, of *The Simpsons* and *South Park*. And so, so much laughter. Still people looked down before catching themselves or lifted up before calling themselves out.

"Why is it so hard to follow those two little rules? Because we want to get it right. Although that perfectionist drive got us all here in the first place, it can also limit our thinking. Perfectionist tunnel vision is so focused on the end it misses opportunities along the way. Not to mention the added stress we heap on ourselves; we do a hundred things right, miss a comma in thing one hundred and one, and that comma is all we remember. But this activity is a chance to quiet that inner perfectionist for a bit and remember how it feels to trust your intuition without worrying about the consequences. There's no way to get this wrong, so stop trying to get it right."

I watched Edward. Again frustration, but now with a playful eye roll. He'd survived falling off the rings and knew it wasn't so bad.

We did two more rounds—one with nondominant hands and humming, one with closed eyes whenever the pen was moving—before it was time for the last piece. One trick I've learned from magicians and psychologists is that getting people to articulate things for themselves can bring abstract feelings into consciousness and make it easier to believe, remember, and repeat later. So to close the activity, I asked everyone to sift through their creations, pick their favorite, and then explain their selection. This is a slight emotional trick because it skips right over the possibility that they may not like these drawings and presumes they agree that each drawing has value.

People talked about lines, feelings, they talked about how the last round was easier than the first because it took that long to relax their perfectionist, others talked about trying to capture the kindness in someone's eyes or the mischief in their smile. One of the things I love about this is that every drawing is a success—just not the success you planned. It doesn't matter that no one's capturing a lifelike portrait; there's always some unexpected beauty. That's a talent in itself—finding unexpected success in failure.

Finally, I close the session with what seems like a simple instruction but is actually very deliberate: "Please give your partners the portraits you made of them."

Since I've had them keep their own work until now, this serves as a chance to reinforce names and faces, to laugh together another time over the drawings, and to essentially exchange gifts. It reinforces their shared experience. Strangers talking and laughing and chatting like old friends. The room was so loud they couldn't hear me begin my closing thank-yous.

But then something interesting happened. Edward clapped his hands for everyone's attention. Then he turned to me. "I actually really loved this. But I notice that you escaped without a single portrait of yourself. Let's rectify that." Sixty seconds later I had twenty portraits of myself.

To this day, my avatar is the sketch Edward did of me that afternoon, a playful reminder of the power of joyful failure.

UNBLINKING LINE: JOYFUL FAILURE

Primary Quality
Resilience

Supporting Themes
Relaxing Perfectionism
Humility
Joy

The What

A deceptively straightforward drawing exercise with rotating partners and a steady stream of playful challenges. The hitch: Everyone fails. And loves doing it.

The How

Partner Up: Everyone is paired up sitting directly across from each other with a paper and Sharpie marker. Then they're given one minute to draw a portrait of their partner. However, there's a catch: They must create their portrait using one continuous line without lifting their pen or looking down at the paper. No lifting up and no looking down.

Repeat for Four Rounds: Then they find a new partner and do it again, but each successive round adds a new element to the two cardinal instructions of no lifting up, no looking down: They must use their nondominant hand; they must smile as big as possible; they must close their eyes whenever they move their pen. Everyone keeps their own art until the end.

Pick Favorites: Finally, everyone looks through their creations, picks their favorite, and then, one by one everyone explains why they picked the one they did. When everyone has shared, open the floor for comments, close with the why, and then have everyone deliver the portraits to their models.

The Why

This activity is a fun, safe way to practice failing together and to practice being intensely focused on something without the promise of success. Not being able to orient ourselves is an opportunity to quiet our inner perfectionist, tamp down our compulsion to self-correct, and just flow with purpose and curiosity. It's an opportunity to remind ourselves what it feels like to focus on the process rather than the product.

This is also a "talent-agnostic" exercise, so it sets everyone on common ground—strangers and friends, interns and CEOs, siblings and spouses. Everyone is welcomed in, no one has the upper hand, and there's beauty in everyone's creation. Rather than hiding the failures, people inevitably proudly hold up their disasters, essentially redefining failure as learning to be shared.

The Materials
Blank printer paper, black markers

GROWTH MINDSET

Pioneered by psychologist Carol Dweck, the growth mindset is an approach to learning that understands strengths as built through effort, not fixed traits. Think back to school: When you aced a test, were you called "smart" or were you a "hard worker"? When you struggled, was it because you were "bad at math" or because you hadn't mastered it *yet*? The growth mindset reframes success and failure as opportunities to learn and grow, showing that achievement comes from persistence, not innate ability.

Dweck's research highlights this: She tested two groups of third graders, praising one for intelligence ("You're so smart!") and the other for effort ("You worked so hard!"). When given a choice between easy and hard tasks, most "smart" kids chose easy ones to maintain their label, whereas "hard workers" opted for the challenge. On a subsequent extra-tough test, the "smart" kids gave up quickly, believing they weren't smart enough, so there was no point in continuing. Nearly 40 percent of the "smart" group then lied about their scores to protect their "smart" identity. "One sentence of intelligence praise put them in the fixed mindset where what they cared most about was looking smart, and where they couldn't cope with challenges. They were being taught to measure themselves by the outcome."[5] The "hard workers," however, believing that effort was the key to their success, kept at it, tried different strategies, persevered.

It takes a tremendous amount of optimism to risk your sense of self. But it's exactly this fear that keeps people from pursuing something that intrigues them or offering an idea that's off the beaten path. Possibilities for contributing our uniqueness to the world get stifled by the fear of failure. That's why a growth mindset is so empowering. It defangs those fears by reframing them as a way to find yourself, rather than lose yourself.

The key, to oversimplify it, is to focus on process, not outcome. That, of course, is easier said than done. That's why we practice failing—to build up our resilience and embrace the explorer inside. If you can adopt a growth mindset, you don't need to fear the outcome because success and failure aren't ends, they're means. They are the tools of growth—endless growth.

FEED ON FAILURE

Even though there are plenty of ways to fail, when I talked with some of the most resilient people I know, there seemed to be a much more focused consensus about what to do when you fail. Two themes stood out:

1. Look differently
2. Learn deeply

LOOK DIFFERENTLY: FINDING A DIFFERENT SUCCESS IN THE FAILURE

My life is covered in Post-it notes. Packing lists, doodle pads, bookmarks, flip books. Not bad for something that was a worthless failure. Originally, 3M was trying to develop glue that would basically adhere until the end of time. It failed. Badly. The team ended up with something a preschooler can pull apart. Failure, they said. Wasted time, they felt. Toss it, they agreed. Except for one person. Inventor Arthur Fry saw the potential for something completely unsought, a solution that would invent an entirely new category of item. It took him ten years to finally convince the rest of the team that this was just a different kind of success, but here we are. There are similar stories about Viagra (failed blood pressure medication), the pacemaker (failed sound recorder), bubble wrap (failed wallpaper), and even YouTube (failed dating app).

Looking differently requires an elasticity of mind that allows you to stretch your point of view beyond the tunnel vision of expectations. That's how you spot a great strategy used for the wrong product, a brilliant line in a stack of clichés, the right person in the wrong job. It's hard. It's humbling. But it makes all the difference.

LEARN DEEPLY: FIND A DIFFERENT PATH TO SUCCESS IN THE FUTURE

From Taylor Swift to wet ducks, the world loves to tell us to shake it off when we fail—and there's wisdom in that. You don't want to lug your failures around, letting them define you forever. But, on the other hand, if you walk away from a failure unchanged, then it truly was for nothing.

One way to practice learning from failure is to learn from the failures of others. At a terrible event? Instead of composing grocery lists or plotting your escape, ask yourself: *Where did they go wrong? Why didn't they notice? How would I fix it?* That way, when you're in a similar spot, you'll be ready to sail over whatever caused them to stumble.

Of course, it's different when it's our own failure.

Failure isn't as good as success—anyone who says otherwise is welcome to my share. But when it hits, don't waste it. Don't focus on blame or excuses; focus on understanding and improving. Don't hide it like a kid with a bad report card. Failure hurts. Let it. Don't deny that you're embarrassed, that you wish it had gone differently. Do something with it. I have a friend whose mantra is "I will succeed, or I will learn." It's that sort of attitude that will let future-you look back at your failures not as setbacks but as slingshots.

Essentially, the idea behind looking differently and learning deeply is that, when you're knocked down, you've got choices. Maybe you use that faceplant moment to admire the grass and see all the bugs and roots you wouldn't have seen if you hadn't been down there. Or you say, "Huh, I got knocked down because I was off balance. Next time I'll set my feet more firmly beneath my center of gravity." But in both cases, you'll get up a slightly better version of yourself.

REWARDING RESILIENCE

Humans hate losing more than they love winning. As a species, we are risk averse. So it's no surprise that fear of failure is the biggest challenge to

"I'm not stuck—I decided to spend the rest of my life here."

psychological safety. Too often, in school, sports, office, and home, mistakes are shameful. We hide them. We shift blame. We pretend we don't care. The biggest opportunity and the hardest challenge is to *genuinely* see the times we blow it as an invitation to improve.

That's easier when the people we admire show us we're valuable even when we fall.

Lip service isn't enough. Organizations can plaster the walls with mottoes and mantras, but if their reward system doesn't match their values, they're not really values—they're PR. If you're looking to build resilience in others, reward the qualities that lead to success, even if they didn't this time around. *Especially* if they didn't this time around. Yes, it's harder to gauge value beyond success, but safety can't grow with an axe hanging over it.

PROTECTIVE PESSIMISM

In a very teenagery kind of way, it's never cool to be disappointed. Even if we feel optimistic, we're conditioned to hide how much we want something. There's a quiet but powerful stigma around disappointment that makes it the perfect gateway to pessimism. People learn to shrug off disappointment with a dismissive, "Meh. I didn't really care about that award / job / date / acceptance letter. No biggie."

Pessimism is repackaged fear. Fear of disappointment. Fear of inadequacy. Fear of failure. Fear that whispers, "This idea won't work. This project will bomb. They'll hate this." Pessimism is fear as a lifestyle. It's an emotional armor many of us embrace after early disappointments to save us the pain, embarrassment, and frustration of believing in something. You can't be disappointed if you didn't expect anything.

But that protection comes at a steep price. You can't truly feel a win when you weren't truly invested in it. It blocks out the light as well as the dark. Although that armor may indeed protect you from some slings and arrows of outrageous fortune, it also traps everything inside just as soft and defenseless as ever. You can't grow if you're locked in your armor. It keeps you small.

Optimism also costs, but it's an investment in yourself.

I am not encouraging rah-rah cheerleading in the face of defeat. I have little patience for that myself. But you don't need pom-poms to want something and work to make it real.

HARD TIMES DELIVER SOLID WORK

In the years that I've been doing this work, countless participants have described how their personal and professional decisions are controlled by fear of failure. So many ideas never took their first breath because success wasn't guaranteed.

One of my favorite experts on ideas whose outcome is very much not guaranteed is Sandy Speicher, former CEO of IDEO. Before moving into the CEO role, Speicher's work as a leader in organizational transformation and global learning was already legendary, using IDEO's design thinking practices to evolve systems of education around the world. When she became CEO, she led IDEO through one of its most difficult periods, facing a pandemic, changing business models, and evolving social mores.

After more than two decades of leading creative teams, departments, and then an entire global organization, Speicher has seen firsthand the pivotal overlap between optimistic persistence and innovative thinking.

"There is a belief out there that designers are constantly optimistic and confident, but that hasn't been my experience," Speicher said. "Creativity isn't all about fun. There can be a lot of fear. Fear of failure. Fear of disappointment. And it's not all in your head. People build up a fear of those risks because they've been hurt before, or they've seen others hurt. Risk doesn't guarantee reward. Acknowledging that allows us to support the profound vulnerability necessary to keep developing creative solutions."[6]

At the crossroads of curiosity and innovation is a dizzying state, where the things you thought you knew—the things that helped you feel stable and clear—are suddenly in question. Speicher calls this disequilibrium. It's actually a very natural state for learning and growth. But that doesn't mean we enjoy it. We crave stability, so disequilibrium can feel incredibly disorienting, frustrating, even offensive. One easy response is to reject the new information and wrap ourselves back up in familiar expectations and understandings. But Speicher has a different suggestion: Learn to sit with the uncertainty.

"I'm human, so of course there's fear about the future," Speicher said. "But if you don't give in to this in-between space, you won't create in the same way. The liminal space allows a unique moment of being open to new possibilities. I know how valuable it is to just be present and allow opportunity to come. Having the precedent helps because I can remind myself of that whenever the fear comes in."

She is a great believer in activities that shake up your perspective and encourage hunting for surprises rather than affirmation. "Confusion, self-doubt, existential searching, getting lost, and then finding your way out of that state of disequilibrium—these are the essential experiences for the emergence of creativity," according to Speicher. Disequilibrium pushes us to dig deeper, ask what we've missed, and engage with the world in new and unexpected ways. Some of the best work comes from the darkest moments. That's why it's so valuable to protect the light of optimism.

PERMISSION TO STRUGGLE

Whether you're raising a child or leading a team, when the ones you're responsible for are up against a real challenge, it's frustrating to sit on your hands. Frustrating, but essential.

"Instead of showing how good you are, how smart you are, how lucky they are to have you," Speicher said, "you slow down, support their development, and bring out their wisdom. My leadership was at its best when I stopped pushing what I believed was right and started asking questions that helped them get there themselves."

However, practical considerations can make it difficult to let others struggle to their own solutions; namely, time and money. Because parents, teachers, and businesses all face external pressure to accomplish things within a timeframe and budget, they often send signals to their charges to cut short those deeper, exploratory stages of creative work and just get it done. This is a recipe for shallow, derivative results. Sometimes urgency is necessary, but if you want the benefits of resilience, allot time and permission to struggle.

Aside from external pressures like time and money, authority figures also have to navigate the internal pressures of guilt and impatience. "Offering a fast answer from your experience is so tempting when someone is struggling," Speicher admitted. "But quick conclusions aren't going to get them to groundbreaking ideas or develop their creative muscles."

And if your team takes a turn you think is a mistake?

"It's really, really tough," Speicher said. "You can guide them. There is the 'What about this? Do you see that? How did you get to there?' approach. But that takes time. You can also just let them fail; sometimes you have to let them find their mistakes in a way that doesn't do lasting damage. But you may not have the luxury of the time and scenarios for those first two. You may need to put a hand in and solve it. Honestly, that may be the best solution sometimes. But even in those circumstances I try to offer a few solutions so they still feel agency."

Whether as a producer or a parent, if you're trying to build someone's resilience, it's crucial they understand that the struggle with disequilibrium is to be expected and respected, even when it leads to dead ends.

AUTHORITY DOESN'T MAKE IT EASIER

As a leader, one clear way to help others navigate failure is to be open about your own. Speicher is extraordinarily generous in this area. She is very frank and vulnerable when talking about the role optimism plays in fueling her own resilience as a leader. "Each time you do something that's higher risk, every time there's potential for greatness, there's potential for equal and opposite loss. Losses all take time to bounce back from and build back from. When you're in a position of authority, it's just as important to be transparent with that part of the process as any other part."

For leaders and caregivers, this may come with an extra layer of anxiety because people need to trust that you'll guide them to safety and success. Will failure lose you their respect? Cost you the admiration of your peers and superiors? Possibly. And that fear leaves many people trapped, feeling like imposters in their own lives. The question is, if people look up to you, is that the example you want to set or would you rather model a different way of being in the world?

OPTIMISM CAN BE LEARNED

Optimism doesn't come easily to everyone. I was raised with that pessimist mindset that would rather be pleasantly surprised than painfully disappointed. My comfort zone was to downplay wins, minimize rejection, and label myself a "realist" in the face of hope.

It's not easy to rewire your neural pathways with new habits and behaviors: one step forward, two steps back, three to the side, stop, drop, and roll. But optimism *can* be learned. It *can* be practiced. Like a muscle, it grows strong with use. Even if it gets away from you for a time, once you've begun the practice, you will always have that emotional muscle memory to return to when you falter and need to build it up again.

One trick is to fuel optimism by mining the precedents. When have you faced something similar? What did you learn? How can you apply that now? If you've been here before, you know you can work your way out again.

Another is to simply notice the moments you choose between optimism and pessimism. Don't adjust your behavior, just notice it. Just say to yourself, "There I go, being pessimistic again." Then move on with your life. That little bit of awareness creates distance between you and the behavior, giving you the space and agency to make different choices when you're ready. Ram Dass called this distance *the witness*. Headspace calls the technique *noting*.

Psychology calls the disruption *cognitive dissonance*. Whatever the name, it's a simple, powerful step toward change.

EXPLANATIONS EXPLAIN A LOT

One thing to begin noticing is how you explain events. Optimists think good things are within their control and the result of their efforts or talents. Pessimists assume good things are beyond their control—controlled by luck or other people. When it comes to bad things, roles reverse: Optimists see them as one-time bumps in an otherwise smooth road, and pessimists tend to blame themselves and see failure as a reflection of their overall worth. This isn't to say optimists avoid responsibility or pessimists can't see their successes, but their framing matters.

As you go through your days, try noting when you give credit to something you can control and when you give credit to something beyond your control. Again, you don't need to force yourself to change anything right away, but just take a moment to notice it before you move on.

OPTIMISM IS RESILIENT

So, yes, optimism gets a bad rap, but it doesn't deserve it. Unlike fluffy positive thinking that leads to daydreaming without action, true optimism opens space to envision new possibilities and delivers the energy and enthusiasm to bring that vision into reality. That's why optimism is the secret sauce for the resilience, persistence, and grit it takes to achieve something worthwhile.

Optimism is about the big picture. It lets you lose a poker hand but stay in the game, lose a battle but continue the war, swing and miss and swing again. I once had an art teacher who would sketch all over my work to show me different techniques. At first, I was frustrated my brilliant piece was being scribbled on. Then I realized his assumption: An artist who learns a lesson will be able to create endlessly, so learning a new technique meant focusing on the hand, not the paper. Optimism shifts your focus from the instance to the practice.

Using safe danger is a great way to build the emotional muscle memory needed to practice optimism and tolerate failure. Activities like Chroma Aroma (see page 206), Memory Floss (see page 237), and Unblinking Line (see page 126) directly target failure and optimism in order to build up resilience and persistence. They pull people off the rings, show them they'll survive a fall so they can practice pushing through uncomfortable moments with grace and confidence.

> ## HABIT BUILDERS
>
> ### Request Rejection
>
> Entrepreneur Jason Comely got to a point in his life where he was paralyzed by a fear of rejection. It was starting to define his life...so he let it. He turned it into a game. "I make myself get rejected at least once every single day by someone." Maybe he asks for a ride across town or a breath mint or a discount from a store. It doesn't matter what it is as long as by the end he can say, "Wow. I disobeyed fear."[7]
>
> Comely sees most of our fears as a story we tell ourselves. A story we can choose to stop repeating. What would it look like to take control of your story for a week and invite one rejection into your life every day?
>
> ### Get Grateful
>
> If rejection is too scary, you can try the flip side of that coin and collect successes. "My days are packed with stress," said Megan Summers, global head of production at Facebook. "So I keep a gratitude journal and write at least a line in it every

night before bed. At first I tried to come up with something new each time, but now I let myself repeat the same things again and again, because I'm still grateful for them." Over time this practice can become a catalog of all the things you can count on—including yourself.

CHAPTER EIGHT

TO FUEL COLLABORATION, INSPIRE CONNECTION

THERE'S A SPECTRUM OF MINDSETS I SEE A LOT IN MY WORK:

<u>Competition</u>　　　<u>Consensus</u>　　　<u>Collaboration</u>

On one end, there's *competition*. This mindset is founded on being better than others. It shows up equally in boardrooms and bake sales, throwing elbows with the assumption that there's not enough success to go around. This is Purpose + Scarcity: If others succeed, you fail. It's a powerful mindset, hard to refuse and defuse. If someone chooses to compete against you, there's little you can do about it.

In the middle is *consensus*, desperate to please everyone by not upsetting anyone. It's Purpose + Conformity. Research shows that the more pressure a team feels to deliver great work, the more that team will tend toward consensus.[1] Pressure makes teams more likely to focus on completing the project than on improving it, a path of least resistance that leads to safe but uninspired outcomes.

At the other end is *collaboration*. Collaboration is a cross-pollination of minds and experience that opens up new insight and potential. People often wax poetic about the benefits of a collaborative culture, but there can be some confusion about what that actually entails, so it's worth taking a moment to clarify. There are plenty of ways to work together—teamwork, tag-teaming, brainstorming. Real collaboration stands apart from those because it's anchored in a trusted connection: Purpose + Connection. A shared sense of purpose drives you all in a common direction, but the connection piece—that's the bit that is misunderstood, underestimated, and ironically, the most essential. *Connection* is shorthand for mutual understanding. You may not agree with each other's choices, but you know each other well enough to understand them. This chapter is all about unpacking how collaboration lives or dies with connection.

CONNECTION MAKES COLLABORATION MORE THAN PROXIMITY

Collaboration takes more than putting people together in a room. Real collaboration needs an environment where it's safe to take risks and get it wrong. It means leveling voices, welcoming everyone, finding common ground and a common language. And that is all work that happens long before anyone arrives in the room.

CONNECTION MAKES COLLABORATION MORE THAN TEAMWORK

Collaboration and *teamwork* are often used interchangeably, but that's selling them each short. Teamwork, like in sports, relies on distinct roles working in sync toward a goal. The quarterback and running back do their own jobs and trust their teammates to do theirs. That's teamwork at its best. And there's a place for that. But it doesn't require the same inputs or produce the same outcomes as collaboration. At its best, collaboration dissolves the divisions that define our responsibilities and lets ideas flow freely. It's a meeting of minds, not roles.

CONNECTION MAKES COLLABORATION MORE THAN TAG-TEAMING

I've heard workplaces describe themselves as collaborative where everyone contributes their part in isolation and then passes it along to the next person. That isn't collaboration—it's a conveyor belt. True collaboration invites constant interplay of skills and perspectives, sparking fresh ideas at every stage. When done with vulnerability, joy, trust, and all the other qualities we've been discussing, collaboration is more than the sum of its parts. It's the difference between a duet and a harmony. Collaboration has a deeper, unexpected resonance. It's not about competition to outdo each other; it's not about conceding to appease each other; you collaborate to fuel each other.

CONNECTION MAKES COLLABORATION MORE THAN COMBINING PREEXISTING THINGS

Everyone bringing their best ideas to the table, fully formed and gift wrapped, isn't collaboration. That's a potluck. Now, potlucks can be wonderful. But the central premise is that the work is already done. You show up with your contribution. Collaboration is different. Collaboration is about everyone going into the kitchen together with their various backgrounds and experience and taste and palates and looking at the ingredients together to make something that none of them could make alone.

CONNECTION MAKES TEAM BUILDING DIFFERENT FROM SKILL BUILDING

Leaders often ask for competitive team-building activities for sales teams, thinking they need to practice competition. I disagree. You've hired these people because they love competition. Kids don't need practice loving candy. They've got it covered. What salespeople really need is the confidence their teammates will have their back, not stab them in it. What they need is help channeling their natural predatory edge to help the organization as a whole—a pack mentality: wolves, not snakes. What they need is connection.

Building meaningful connection can be tricky between competitive people; but tricky doesn't mean impossible. I've found the most useful thing I can do is help them share the last thing they want to: weakness. Activities

"Let's show those jerks from Accounts Payable that no one collaborates better than Accounts Receivable!"

like Super Secret (see page 16) and Homegrown Heroes (see page 93) are great for this because they normalize imperfection and even let people turn vulnerability into a kind of competition (if they must).

The trick is getting the group to take it seriously. You wouldn't think being silly would be scary, but playfulness can feel threatening to people who treasure their polished personas. Competitive teams faced with something fun often blow it off, make jokes, and act like the cool kids in the back of the class making it clear to anyone in earshot that this is beneath them. I short-circuit that behavior as much as possible, but there's one thing that makes a difference like nothing else: leadership. When the boss shows up, models good behavior, and makes the expectations clear, people fall into line. Every pack needs a leader to show them the way—especially when the way is unfamiliar and uncomfortable.

One leader explained it beautifully: "The session helped us feel the difference between competing *with* each other and competing *against* each other."

ACTIVITY

Emblemottos

A remote team of ten very different people stare back at me through their screens as I lay out the instructions:

*Think about the year ahead and come up with a motto for yourself that encapsulates how you'd like to grow—personally, not professionally—over the next twelve months. This isn't a New Year's resolution. No "go to the gym" or "eat less ice cream after midnight." This should be something positive, aspirational, the bumper sticker slogan that expresses how would you like to show up in the world a little better, and **better** can mean whatever you want it to.*

> **Your Motto Can Be Straightforward:** Get back in touch with nature.
> **Or Philosophic:** Go slow to go fast.
> **Encouraging:** The muse comes during creation, not before.
> **Or Reflective:** Strong opinions, lightly held.

Write yours down, but don't share it yet.

Ten sets of eyes around the world stare off into space, measuring the distance between where they are and where they'd like to be, formulating a signpost to point them in the right direction.

While they ponder, I continue:

Any business book or self-help book will tell you that, if you've got a goal, the first step is to write it on a Post-it and slap it on your monitor so you'll see it every day. What they tend to ignore is that the second step is to utterly ignore that Post-it, because work piles up, the dog needs to be walked, the kids have set their socks on fire. For most of us, self-care usually gets pushed to the bottom of the to-do list. So with that in mind, this activity is a gentle way to help your goal keep its head above water when life floods in.

*In a moment you're all going to anonymously swap mottoes, and I'd like you to make a gift for the author of the motto you receive: You're going to have twenty-five minutes to create a virtual collage that brings their motto to life, a visual manifestation of their goal that can serve as a vibrant, joyful, colorful beacon reminding them of what's important **to them**.*

At the mention of creativity, the blood drains from about half the faces. This I'm used to.

I want to emphasize that this is not about your artistic prowess. You're not expected to set the art world on fire. No matter how creative or uncreative you've labeled yourself, this is more about empathy than artistry. What is important is your intention, your thoughtfulness, that you really consider what's going to help them, what they need. Also, because this is anonymous, you can't tailor it to their likes. You just have to trust your instincts. That's part of the gift—you're sharing your vision, insight, and interpretation with them. That's what makes it meaningful.

They seem skeptical, but calm. That's good enough.

I introduce the library of images I've curated for them—panthers, peacocks, galaxies, flaming Corvettes, disco balls with angel wings—fuel for their creativity.

Over the next twenty-five minutes, I play Bowie and Beyoncé and watch skepticism melt into focus. Some scoop up images like contestants in grocery game shows who clear a whole shelf at once. Others attack with surgical precision, one image at a time, first the T. rex, then the toothpick in its claws, then the ruby-red sunglasses. I asked them to leave their audio on, so we hear babies crying, dogs barking, keys clacking. The spontaneous sounds of life around the world prompt chuckles from fellow parents and questions from pet fans.

Twenty-five minutes goes too fast for everyone, but that's by design. No time for perfectionism, just instinct and intuition.

Then we come to the sneakiest part of the activity: the share back. We do the share back in two beats, first hearing from the creator of the image and then from the writer of the motto. It's sneaky because they think they're talking about these creations, but what they're really revealing are their values, their priorities, their perspective on life, all without realizing it.

The motto Sunil received was "What no longer serves is no longer needed." The image he created featured a parade of iridescent insects, mollusks, and reptiles marching up a mountain of discarded shells—shadows of themselves that multiply like echoes across the page. There are also vibrantly colorful birds pecking their way out of eggs and, finally, at the head of the parade, a child's silhouette leaping into the air from a pile of knight's armor, reaching for the string of a red balloon.

"Wow," whispers Jenna, the motto writer. "It's not at all what I had in mind when I wrote it, but it's perfect." She explains that her motto comes from a desire to recalibrate her life and focus on what truly matters. She says she especially loves the imagery of the animals who outgrow their skin, because when she wrote her motto, she was inclined to villainize the parts that she no longer wants in her life. "Even though I don't love bugs, they're reminding me you need different things at different times to get you through. I should probably be kinder with myself about past choices."

I ask, "Are you comfortable sharing why this motto is important to you *now*?" After a moment of hesitation she explains that she's always given 110 percent to work, but now she has a family. "I'm too stressed and exhausted at the end of the day to be the parent I want to be. It's time for a change."

"My motto is, Say No to Say Yes!" announces Patrick. "For the same reason. I need boundaries before there's nothing left of me."

They all seem surprised and delighted that there is such overlap in their perspectives. I'm delighted, but not surprised. Whenever I run activities that surface what people want more of in life, certain themes emerge again and again that really bring home how universal some of our struggles are:

Authenticity ("Unapologetically me," "Bring your unique magic")
Balance ("Everything in proportion," "Stress is a choice")
Boundaries ("Don't set yourself on fire to keep others warm," "Time for me")
Community ("Reach out and reconnect," "Prioritize people")
Creativity ("Spark joy," "Make room for wonder")
Empathy ("Less judgment, more forgiveness," "Walk their walk")
Expectations ("Set your own goal post," "Don't let the uncontrollable control me")
Forgiveness ("Let it go," "Understanding is overcoming")
Gratitude ("Appreciate the little things," "Collect happy moments")
Health ("Be mindful of mindfulness," "Food isn't feeling")
Imposter Syndrome ("Trust the voice inside and let it sing," "You are everything you need")
Priorities ("Be present in the now," "Focus on what matters")
Realistic Standards ("Be kinder to myself," "Progress, not perfection")
Risk-Taking ("Take the leap," "Breathe in courage, breathe out fear")
Slowing Down ("Protect your calm," "Take a breath. Repeat.")

Time and again someone will share something they worry is too unprofessional, only to hear from their audience that everyone feels something similar but hadn't actually registered it to themselves until hearing it articulated.

After Jenna has thanked Sunil, we move on to hear about the image she created for the motto "Shine from the inside out." One by one, we go around until everyone has given and everyone has received.

EMBLEMOTTOS: GOALS MADE VISIBLE

Primary Quality
Connection

Supporting Themes
Problem-Solving
Vulnerability
Trust

The What

A talent-agnostic opportunity to create a meaningful gift for a colleague that helps them grow into their best selves.

The How

Reflect: Everyone writes down a motto for themselves that encapsulates how they'd like to grow as a person (not professionally) in the year ahead. Swap these mottos anonymously so that no one knows whose is whose.

Create: Everyone gets twenty-five minutes to make a gift for the author of the motto they've received: a visualization of that motto. If you're in-person, use crafting materials. If you're remote, collage with images.

Share: For each creation, the share back happens in two beats. First, hear from the crafter about what they've created. Second, hear from the motto writer about why they've chosen that motto. The facilitator or group can ask some gentle probing questions to get to the why behind the motto they've written (Why this motto now? What's going to be the biggest challenge? What's the first step you're going to take?). Then the motto writer shifts into the creator role and shares what they created for the motto they received. That motto writer in turn shares why they've chosen their motto. And so on until every gift and motto have been shared. Open the floor for comments, then close out by sharing the why.

The Why

Articulating goals is one of the most powerful first steps to reaching them. Unspoken, unshared goals are easy to postpone, neglect, and forget. The gift of these emblems is that they're a fun way to keep that motto front and center, keep it from being completely crowded out and forgotten in the pressures of the day-to-day. And it's also a lovely bonding experience to both give and receive an unexpected gift.

Emblemottos is designed to help us think about our purpose, crystalize our goals, and better understand the goals and motivations of the people around us. It helps us see the people we are beneath the roles we normally play. Having someone else create your emblem for you allows them to surprise you with what they see in your thinking, which can reveal unexpected nuances or unseen dimensions to further inspire you. The gift-giving aspect creates an opportunity for people to inspire each other, cultivate a deeper investment in their peers, and reveal the richness of the workplace community.

Materials

In-Person: Imagine a kindergarten art room. Pipe cleaners, pom-poms, googly eyes, markers, popsicle sticks, fabrics, felts, mirrors, gem stickers, beads, feathers, string, disposable coffee cups, air-dry clay, balloons, wooden blocks, anything else within reach

Glue guns, scissors, tape, markers

Online: Collaborative slide deck or whiteboard; collection of about a hundred beautiful images (from nature, from technology, from bodies, from faces, from history, from culture, from space, from animals, from architecture, from food, and so forth)

THE GIFT OF CONNECTION

Although the Emblemottos activity might feel light and playful, a number of deeper levels of connection are at work. First, there is the self-connection that comes from taking inventory, crystalizing a goal, and then committing to it publicly. Articulating goals is a crucial step toward reaching them. Unshared goals are easy to postpone, but this is a vibrant way to give the big picture a voice instead of allowing it to be shouted down by day-to-day pressures.

Second, a daisy chain of one-to-one connections builds up between everyone and the person from whom they received a gift and the person for whom they created one. Everyone gets to have their vision played back through someone else's eyes.

Finally, there's the group connection, because they've opened up deeper conversations than the typical chitchat about weekend plans. Instead, everyone has heard what everyone else is carrying behind their professional facade, what they're striving for and struggling with, and that understanding strengthens the underlying layer of meaningful connection that we all need to do our best work and help others to do theirs.

This isn't just a Hallmark card sentiment; it's backed by data and research. Cigna reports that lonely workers take two times more sick days, are three times more dissatisfied with their jobs, and are 25 percent less efficient.[2] Meanwhile, workers who feel genuinely connected to their peers are four times more effective and efficient and can better communicate, collaborate, and coordinate.[3] Imagine yourself or your workforce accomplishing four times as much.[4] On a personal level, connecting with your community lowers anxiety, decreases depression, elevates self-esteem, deepens empathy, strengthens the immune system, and may even increase longevity by 50 percent.[5]

By the end, the team has a greater understanding of each other's strengths and struggles. With the team I worked with, I later heard they began weekly check-ins using one Emblemotto as a focal point to see how not just the writer but also everyone in the group was faring with that particular issue. They still only see each other through screens, but they say the screens now feel more like windows.

THE GIFT OF GIVING

Inspiration should be a circuit. Receiving it is only the first half of the cycle. Take it in, add a bit of yourself, put it back into the world transformed. We spend our lives absorbing stimuli from the world through books, art, conversation, nature, internet, TV. That inspiration needs somewhere to go or it stagnates. We can't tell our stories to our toes or share our photographs with the wind. We're social animals and no matter how independent we may feel, the way we value our role in the world is deeply tangled in the value we provide to other people. That's why I so often build an exchange into my activities. Generosity can be a fast lane to connection because the act of giving is powerful for both sides of the gift.

In my experience, people are more intentional about things they make for others compared to things they make for themselves. One reason Emblemottos works so well is that it's framed as a gift. Gift giving fosters a sense of generosity and caregiving that is a more powerful bonding agent than most people realize.

People often resist giving more of themselves for fear of imbalance. "What if I give and get nothing back? What if I'm left without? Why on earth should I risk it?"

Because it will make you happier.

Yale psychology professor Laurie Santos says the three things proven to consistently improve happiness are sleep, gratitude, and helping other people. She should know; her course, "The Science of Wellbeing," is one of the most popular in Yale's history, having been taken by 3.3 million people to date. I can't do much for your sleep habits beyond saying that you probably aren't getting enough. But the other two factors, gratitude and other people, that's a different story.

PUSHOVER PUSHBACK

A quick note on generosity: There's a fine line between savior and sucker. If you naturally gravitate toward kindness, your first reaction to someone's struggles may be to offer a hand. And kudos to you. You're one of the good ones. Keep it up. But at the same time, keep an eye out. Be a lifeguard, not a crossing guard. The lifeguard leaps into action in a crisis, whereas the crossing guard is always vigilant so that others don't have to be. Whether it's money, time, or just a sympathetic ear, it's oh-so-easy for good intentions to leave you used up and leave them useless. Luckily, patterns of dependency follow a pretty consistent trajectory.

Five Steps to Dependency

1. *Appreciation:* The recipient feels grateful for your kindness. We like this stage. This is a good, healthy stage.
2. *Anticipation:* They start hoping for more help. The slippery slope begins. You still give, but it feels less like a choice.
3. *Expectation:* They plan on your support. You feel obligated not to let them down.
4. *Entitlement:* They feel you owe them help. They're angry and resentful if you don't deliver.
5. *Dependency:* They rely on you. They feel helpless and you feel responsible for solving their problems.

I've been on both ends of this pattern—whether receiving financial help from my parents or giving homework help to my kids—and breaking it is never easy. It may take setting boundaries, fostering self-reliance, or even seeking professional guidance. But one thing is for sure: The earlier you spot it and address it, the better.

ACTIVE GENEROSITY

There's an irony to the fact that the best way to satisfy yourself is to satisfy others. Parents, volunteers, anyone who's ever given a really thoughtful gift—they all know this. Sharing your talents in service of others is the most powerful way to feel the value of what you have to offer. The flip side of generosity is, of course, gratitude, and I design activities like Hour Gift to You (see page 223), Towering Inspiration (see page 249), and Expert-Tease (see page 212) to intertwine them, so everyone can model and experience both. Because it's this dynamic of authentic generosity and genuine gratitude that so often nurtures that most elusive of relationship traits: loyalty.

TEA CAKE MINDSET

We all carry within our souls a pantheon of role models. The giants whose shoulders we hope one day to be worthy to perch upon. Jane Goodall. Jane Austen. Neil deGrasse Tyson. Neil Patrick Harris. Mr. Rogers. Miss Piggy. Whether it's the way they handled adversity, perfected their craft, or lived their values, their particular radiance lights our path toward the person we hope we might someday be. One of the brightest stars in my pantheon is my aunt Anstice.

Anstice spent much of her career as a New York caterer, serving clients from elementary schools to Paul Newman. When I first came to New York for grad school, I hit one of my lifetime lows and hid away in my shoebox apartment, broke, lost, and depressed. But Anstice swooped in, got me into therapy, showed me the town, and put me to work as a cater waiter. That's when I discovered the power of tea cake.

On every job, Anstice brought a tea cake just for the staff to nibble on. Was this a life-changing baked good? No. It was Entenmann's. But this small gesture was emblematic of how Anstice chose to move through the world. Yes, she paid fairly, but more than this, she treated people with kindness, respect, and generosity. (The tea cake was one small gesture among many more significant ones, but I have a relentless sweet tooth so it's one of my favorites.)

Graduate school ain't cheap, so I wore my indestructible polyester tuxedo for a number of different catering companies in addition to Anstice's. The difference was stunning. With Anstice, staff arrived early, stayed late, laughed and smiled, and always, always—this was the most telling—reached for the heaviest thing first. Always. Everyone. Generosity just permeated the entire experience.

I worked with those same people for other companies; companies that checked their watches, regulated breaks, and certainly didn't provide tea cake. Transactional leadership inspires transactional followers. You get what you pay for, not one whit more. Both sides suspect the other, afraid of being cheated. The same staff who gave their all for Anstice gave the minimum for the others. At the end of the night, they stacked a chair or two and headed for the subway. Transaction complete.

Anstice utterly refuses to live a transactional life. She goes out of her way to make others feel seen and appreciated—ice water for mail carriers on sweaty days, hot tea in the winter so her housekeeper can refresh herself. She has performed big kindnesses on an amazingly regular basis—but you don't need to nurse someone back to health to earn their loyalty. These little kindnesses, the thoughtful, unexpected generosity that wouldn't have been missed, make all the difference precisely because they wouldn't have been missed. They were a choice. An effort just to make someone's life a little better. When it's authentic and offered without strings, that's the sort of generosity that invites real loyalty.

I was raised in a home marked by scarcity—an ingrained fear there would never be enough, and if there happened to be enough at the moment, something would soon change that. So part of me initially assumed Anstice's abundance mindset was founded on...well...abundance. I couldn't imagine an outlook like this had dealt with scarcity. I was very wrong. Some of the stories of her life are marvelous (dancing till dawn at Studio 54, homesteading on a Long Island onion farm, filming epics in the Rajasthan desert, a whirlwind romance with a dashing German baron), but many are less so. Very much less so. Out of respect for her privacy, I will only say that many people would have emerged from certain chapters of her life as bitter, angry, and cynical people. I certainly would have.

But Anstice did not. She tells me that those feelings were there, of course. But once she had some breathing room from these difficult situations, she decided that life was too precious to waste living in darkness. Which I find remarkable enough. But what earned her a spot in my pantheon is not just how she chooses to live her life but how much, big and small, she brings to the lives of others.

LOYALTY BEGETS LOYALTY

People notice when you expect loyalty without offering any yourself. You can buy compliance or scare people into obedience, but loyalty has to be earned. Why? Because it's emotional. Some argue that loyalty is just self-preservation by another name, because if you're part of a group, you want that group to be strong. Like cheering for your alma mater. But in a strange way, loyalty goes against self-preservation. It's defending someone at the risk of your own standing. It's refusing a better offer because you feel invested in your current situation. Loyalty is not cheering along when things are going well; it's standing firm when things are a shambles. Loyalty is irrational in the most human of ways.

I've lost count of how many times clients have said they want to build loyalty by offering perks and bonuses. But that's not loyalty—it's bribery. And bribes leave you vulnerable to anyone with bigger perks or sexier bonuses walking away with your people. I've worked for companies that expect loyalty but offer none in return. They ladle out the shiny things when things are good, but when challenges hit, people find themselves disposable. Perks are nice, but they carry no emotional weight if the care they're meant to represent evaporates when times get tough. Layoffs, though sometimes necessary, don't destroy loyalty as much as hypocrisy does. When leaders who are cutting jobs still give themselves bonuses, you can be sure whoever's left behind will notice. If you don't stand by your people, don't expect them to stand by you.

"And for just an additional ice pop per week you can upgrade to my Best Buddies Plus plan."

To be clear, I'm not saying businesses should start the day with hugs or dole out perks until the coffers are bare. That's ridiculous. The realities of business are the realities of business, and profit margins can be razor thin. I'm also not saying that unbridled generosity is the only way to inspire dedicated, hardworking employees. But if it's loyalty you're after, loyalty is a different beast.

Business may not be personal, but loyalty is. Loyalty grows because people feel like they matter to you. Feel cared for. Feel you have their best interests at heart. Loyalty is not transactional; it's emotional.

CONNECTION IS BIGGER THAN SMALL TALK

Nourishing a collaborative community means satisfying ego without feeding it. It's not a place where everyone gets a participation trophy but is rather a place where everyone feels that participating is the trophy. People need to feel valuable. Competitive communities encourage a scarcity mentality—there's not enough to go around, so you better earn it or you're gone. The healthier mindset for a collaborative community is one of abundance—the sun can warm us all equally.

Real collaboration is when the many hands of multiple perspectives uncover problems and possibilities that would have been missed. It's when seasoned experts and enthusiastic newcomers inspire each other and raw ideas can be shared with the confidence that others can refine them. It's not about working with each other but about *fueling* each other. Collaboration requires trust, respect, and generosity because, at its heart, connection is about understanding. It's learning why someone does what they do, wants what they want, thinks what they think. Connection doesn't mean you agree, but it does mean there's a bridge between your differences that allows your worlds to mingle and inspire each other.

A collaborative community—whether it's work, home, or the neighborhood book club—thrives on welcoming, common ground where everyone feels both entitled and enabled to share. Safe danger activities like Emblemottos (see page 147), Head in the Game (see page 219), and Moving Stories (see page 31) focus on the qualities that build connection and can help move you away from the familiarity of competition and the safety of consensus toward the impact of meaningful collaboration.

HABIT BUILDER

The Whites of Their Eyes

I once held the door for someone at a coffee shop—nothing heroic—but the guy looked me straight in the eyes and said "thank you" as he walked by. In a light and silly way it made me feel seen and appreciated. Again, I wasn't saving anyone's life, I was just letting him go first, but I liked the feeling, and so ever since, I do my best to follow his example: I look people in the eyes when I thank them. When someone hands me my mail, my coffee, a menu. Thank you with eye contact. When someone holds the elevator, the subway, the door. Thank you with eye contact. If you already do this, you may be thinking, what's the big deal? But it's so much easier to shout "thanks!" over your shoulder that being intentional about human-to-human connection is actually a pretty rare thing.

Try it at least once a day for a week and see how people react.

CHAPTER NINE

TO BUILD COMMUNITY, INSPIRE TRUST

SHINY HAPPY PEOPLE

"We have a stellar community...except for the people." I've heard that sentiment disguised in a zillion euphemisms. They complain of groups that don't connect, don't trust, stick in silos, cling to what they know or how they've always done it. People want healthy, happy communities, but the other people keep getting in the way.

What makes a healthy, happy community? We've touched on joy, vulnerability, curiosity, optimism, and connection. But this chapter is perhaps the most important because it's about the quality that supports all those and unlocks myriad others: trust. Trust is the bridge between a "me" mindset and an "us" worldview.

When I joined IDEO after a career in financial institutions, labor unions, higher education, news publications, market research, movie studios, food service, and graphic design, I was shocked. I'd worked with kind, curious, talented people before—but usually as rare islands surrounded by indifference, greed, and pettiness. Never had I found a culture where fun, inspiring, purpose-driven people were the *norm*. I'm sure there are other places like this out there. Lord, I hope so. But for me, this was a first.

Visitors shook their heads and talked about how lucky we were to work in a creative industry, how they envied the collaborative environment, our permission to be curious. But I'd been in creative industries, collaborative environments, and curious cultures. This was different. The heart of this community was not actually creativity, collaboration, or even curiosity. The heart of the community was trust.

What really made that workplace sing was that these very different people, with different backgrounds and different goals, fundamentally trusted each other. With their best ideas. With their worst. With their time and talents, with their blood, sweat, and tears (I can give you dates where I contributed all three). Sure, there were disagreements, but even then, they assumed good. Critiques weren't feared judgments but were help to make the work better. It was a culture that valued not just our professional roles but also the humans behind them. People first. People with strengths and flaws, fears and hopes, hearts and history. That personal connection fueled professional excellence.

THE LONELINESS EPIDEMIC

For a busy professional, a happy community might feel like a pleasant perk, like an espresso machine or live plants. For a busy person, it might feel like an "add it to the list" sort of goal, right between getting to the gym and less screen time. According to the latest Science (capital S), that's outdated thinking. Connection, it turns out, is not a fluffy nice-to-have. Connection has a direct impact on our productivity, health, mental capacity, and life span.

Life. Span.

As much as I value connection, I have a hard time placing it in the life-or-death category. But, apparently, I'd be wrong. As I touched on earlier, no less than Dr. Vivek Murthy, the former surgeon general of the United States, has been sounding the alarm for years. Loneliness, he says, isn't just a bummer feeling we should grow up and get over; it's a national health crisis. Loneliness raises the risk of heart disease, dementia, stroke, depression, and anxiety; it increases the risk of premature death to equal that of smoking daily.[1]

"Social connection is as fundamental to our mental and physical health as food, water, and sleep," Dr. Murthy said. Yet one in two adults reports feeling lonely.

Note the careful word choice: *reports*. Imagine how many stiff-upper-lip, can-do, pull-it-together people chose not to acknowledge a silly weakness of character like loneliness. Except it's not a silly weakness of character.

Lack of connection isn't just bad for minds and bodies; it's also bad for business. Dr. Murthy points out that, "at work, loneliness reduces task performance, limits creativity, and impairs other aspects of executive function such as reasoning and decision making."[2] Meanwhile, workforces that feel connected are more fulfilled, productive, and engaged and less likely to experience illness, injury, and burnout.

Dr. Murthy's research points to four basic actions to overcome isolation:

- *Connect* (Answer a phone call from a friend.)
- *Share* (Invite someone over to share a meal.)
- *Listen* (Be present during conversation.)
- *Serve* (Seek out opportunities to serve others.)

"These steps may seem small," he acknowledges, "but they are extraordinarily powerful."[3]

So, what's the problem? Get hopping.

But of course it's not that easy. I'll be honest, I read his article in 2017. I shared it. Discussed it. And then did absolutely nothing differently. You know why? Because it takes a lot of effort to change behaviors. You need to have a goal, make a plan, execute the plan, stay with it when the novelty wears off. That's why we make the same slate of resolutions every New Year's. Knowing what and why we should change doesn't mean we will.

As it happens, 2017 is also when I was chatting with a colleague about how much I loathed typical team-building activities, and, with a well-timed side-eye, he nudged me to come up with something better, something that would be both fun and worthwhile. Two weeks later, I gathered our studio for my first activity, Conceptual Candies (see page 208).

I took my colleague's nudge to heart because I didn't want to be that guy who complains without offering solutions. I had no aspirations beyond trying to live up to my own standards. But that's when I saw how powerful creative play can be when it's wielded with a slight edge. I saw how it lowered the bar for engagement and made it easy to give it a try. I saw how people's creations reflected their individual voice and thought process. I saw how people who thought they were just talking about their creation were really sharing their values, their perspectives, their anxieties, and their hopes.

One of the problems with behavior change is our need for instant gratification. These things take time, but even though we may be well on our way, if we can't see progress, we give up. That's what's nice about self-contained activities, such as the safe danger activities. They mitigate that disappointment, because there is both short-term gain (dopamine, connection, recognition) and the option for long-term change (opening new connections, conversations, and avenues of trust). The safe danger aspect provides a way to wrestle with blocks, defuse emotional booby traps, practice behaviors, and put values into action. But without actually committing. It's like a free sample. A taste of what's possible.

"Happy hours, coffee breaks, and team-building exercises are designed to build connections between colleagues, but do they really help people develop deep relationships?" Dr. Murthy asked, before pointing out that "real connection requires creating an environment that embraces the unique identities and experiences of employees inside and outside the workplace."[4]

"We really appreciate the way you bring nothing of yourself to the office."

Creative safe danger elevates team building to that level by helping people practice trust in meaningful, approachable ways.

ACTIVITY

Skin in the Game

They turned the corner and stopped silent in their tracks. They'd been chatting happily—designers, coders, directors, and coordinators—enjoying the stretch in their legs after a long morning and curious about what the free lunch and team-building activity would offer. But instead of our normal, noisy café, they faced a dark, mysterious wall. Too tall to see over and running the length of the space, the pitch-black partition was broken only by elbow-high mouse holes and a few lines of large white text stenciled in the center:

BEHIND THIS WALL ARE ARTISTS WITH TEMPORARY TATTOO INK.
THE INK WILL LEAVE AN IMAGE ON YOUR SKIN FOR AT LEAST THREE WEEKS.
WE INVITE YOU TO PLACE YOUR ARM THROUGH THE OPENING AND LET THE ARTIST TATTOO YOU.

NO REQUESTS. NO RESTRICTIONS. NO TALKING.
TRUST US.

Nervous shuffling and excited laughter. Some took the risk, warily rolling up sleeves, placing an arm through the hole, smiling as they felt ink and touch. Some did not, hemming and hawing, reading and re-reading the words.

The talented, thoughtful artists behind the partition had been asked to draw something that evoked trust for them. Some drew elegant geometric patterns that signified the balance of trust, others made ornate illustrations representing the feelings of being trusted or cared for, one wrote *trust* in Morse code—the dots and lines creating a mysterious and beautiful rhythm on the skin. Each was unique.

The whole group talked afterward about their tattoos, discussing the risk, the surprise, the helplessness, the unknown. But the heart of the activity is less about the tattoo itself than the moment of decision. The moment when you had to take stock of your emotional inventory and ask: Do I have enough trust to put my skin in the hands of a mystery? That was the reflection I wanted to spark, the awareness I hoped would be useful. Because, for me, trust is the unsung linchpin of being our best selves.

SKIN IN THE GAME: BRAVERY TATTOO

Primary Quality
Trust

Supporting Themes
Risk-Taking
Vulnerability
Optimism

The What

Trust a stranger to tattoo you. Participants get a temporary tattoo without any input or restrictions.

The How

Prep: You need two key elements to pull this off: mystery and talent. So, line up artists who are worth people's trust, artists who will gift people with an image that they can enjoy. Then figure out the logistics for your space. You'll need to create some sort of barrier that visually separates the artists from the participants but that allows people to stick their arm through to get the tattoo.

Keep Quiet: Post the instructions and refuse to say anything more:

Behind this wall are artists with temporary tattoo ink.
The ink will leave an image on your skin for at least three weeks.
We invite you to place your arm through the opening and let the artist tattoo you.

No requests. No restrictions. No talking.
Trust us.

Share: Let everyone show off their tattoo and share their thought process throughout the experience: Whether they participated or abstained, how did they come to their decision? Was it an easy or hard decision? How do they feel about it now? Open the floor for comments, then close out by sharing the why.

The Why

We all have a narrative in our heads of who we are. Do we welcome risks or embrace safety? Do we see the unknown as threat or adventure? This activity creates a moment of decision that lets us put that narrative to the test. How much risk is too much? How little information is too little for trust? Then, for the next few weeks everyone will have this lovely reminder of the moment when they asked themselves: Do I have enough trust to put my skin in the hands of a mystery?

The Materials

Barrier (I've used testing privacy shields, pipe and drape, foam core, curtains, etc.)

Temporary tattoo ink (We used Jagua, but there are plenty of varieties.)

THE PRIVATE LIFE OF TRUST

It's tempting to give up on trust. Hypocritical leaders, cheating partners, flawed celebrities—the world makes it really easy to justify the skepticism many of us use to protect ourselves from disappointment. But, as with any shield, protecting yourself limits yourself. To show up in the world as your full, authentic self—the self that's not constrained by conformity, that's not wearing the ill-fitting behaviors of others, that's guided by a sense of unique purpose—means trusting yourself in the hands of others.

This trust isn't about leaving your laptop unattended or checking your kids' browser history. It's the trust it takes to risk being different: different from those with power over you, different from those you admire, even different from the person you're told to be if you want to be loved.

How often does the world hear, "I write songs / stories / poems, but I'd be embarrassed to share them." How many people secretly dream of learning carpentry or of flying lessons or of a new hairstyle? People blame shyness or insecurity, but beneath all the dust those dreams gather year after year is a lack of trust—trust that you'll be supported, not silenced; that your dreams won't be dismissed or demeaned; that the people around you won't shame you back into your lane. To feel authentic, to feel free, you can't be ashamed of the things that make your heart sing.

The irony of this—that our sense of individuality is fed by our relationships with others—is not lost on me. But take it up with your brain, I'm just the messenger.

Now, obviously, you shouldn't just trust everyone. (Your kids are 1,000 percent looking at stuff that would horrify you, and the tattooed hipster sipping chai at the next table over is not a reliable laptop theft deterrent if you need to use the bathroom.) That's not trust, that's lazy naivete. Trust needs to be built by both sides, simultaneously, symbiotically. Trust takes effort. Trust takes time. Trust is a risk. And that effort, time, and risk may not feel worth it—especially if you've been burned before.

Happily, there's good evidence that says it's worth it. Research shows that adults who build trusting connections where they feel safe, seen, and valued tend to have lasting relationships, stronger self-esteem, and the confidence to share feelings and seek support. Whether it's a romantic partner or professional partner, the worse the parts of yourself you can share, the more progress you can make together. Like any bridge, trust entails risk—but it's also how you get to where you want to be.

There's a sort of chicken and egg question about trust and qualities like feeling safe, seen, and valued. But which comes first doesn't matter. Those qualities need to be in place to create that trust, but at the same time, if you're not open to that trust in the first place, those qualities can't work their magic. So, in the spirit of that great quote, "The muse comes during the act of creation, not before," you can say, "Trust comes during the act of trusting, not before."

You can cultivate trust with partners, family, old friends, new friends, neighbors, peers, or all of the above. Where it happens isn't as important as *that* it happens so you can explore the full potential of who you are and what you have to offer. Trust enough to share; share enough to trust.

You can't make everyone like you. You can't build love. But you can build trust.

TRUST AT WORK

Trust is a strangely overlooked quality. Colleagues can be smart, fun, serious. Friends will have your back, make you laugh, get you. Rarely are coworkers or pals described as trustworthy. It sounds grandiose. A little too emotional. A little too vulnerable. Perhaps because it implies that you have things fragile enough to require trust. Yet trust is the foundation for any genuine connection or meaningful collaboration.

I've often found that when organizations struggle to build a strong community, the real issue isn't imagination or participation—it's trust. But why? Why is trust so crucial? Two reasons: bad questions and bad answers.

RISKING BAD QUESTIONS

There's a great line in a Sherlock Holmes story: "There is nothing more deceptive than an obvious fact."[5] The obvious goes unquestioned since it's, duh, obvious. The problem is that obvious doesn't mean true. Obviously, the sun moves across the sky. Obviously, people aren't just going to rent out their homes to strangers. Obviously, the Macarena is an awesome dance. It's only when we risk questioning the obvious that we can think outside the parameters of convention and see a vast world of new possibilities.

In hindsight, it's easy to differentiate between questions that were pointless and ones that were prescient. But in the moment, it's not so clear. So, what makes the difference between a team stuck in old mindsets and teams who push the boundaries? Confidence that the people around you understand your worth so you've got the flexibility to take risks, stumble, even question the obvious, and still be respected and valued. Without that in place, people are naturally concerned with putting their best foot forward, worrying about their reputation, and protecting their bonuses.

You probably don't want to feel dumb. Few people line up for that. But trust allows you to ask honest, probing, dumb questions about other people's ideas without you feeling embarrassed or them feeling judged. That's important because their idea may not be as brilliant as they think it is, but your question may improve it. Or, if it is brilliant, there's no better way to grow than to get curious about why you're missing what everyone else seems to get.

The trust to ask bad questions is crucial. If no one questioned the way it's always been done, we'd never have invented the wheel, much less the cappuccino. There's nothing more generous and helpful than a teammate willing to look stupid with a bad question.

RISKING BAD ANSWERS

One way to gauge trust is by how bad an idea you're willing to share. You can be vulnerable without having trust, but you can't have trust without vulnerability. And it's so important to share bad ideas, because if you're really trying something original, your worst ideas may lead to your best.

People cannot understand something truly original. I'm not being cynical. I mean literally—if it's too far from the familiar, it's gibberish. It's madness. Your brain literally can't invent something out of nothing but can only mix, match, and mush parts of life it has experienced. Any new idea the brain encounters needs to be contextualized within the realm of the familiar. Something too far from the known takes time to process.

Your best ideas may only make sense to you at first because they come from your unique experience, perspective, history, from where you've been, what you've seen, how you've felt.

But what confuses others initially may turn out to be extraordinary once they understand. Likewise, when others trust you, they can bring new, raw material to the table that you may have the skills to shape. That's why being comfortable sharing ideas that deviate from the norm is so critical for innovation. When you can trust others with your worst ideas, your embarrassing stories, your cherished memories, you expand the space where ideas can grow and enrich the nourishment that feeds them.

Then again, your ideas may be terrible. That happens. Be okay with it. Trust creates an environment where you can take risks and surprise yourself, but if your worst ideas are stifled by mistrust, your best ideas may also be lost in the silence.

"Anyone want to build on Larry's stupid idea?"

SPEAKING OUT LOUD

I've spoken with many people about why they don't speak up. Often, it's fear of saying the wrong thing or assuming someone else has already thought of it—classic imposter syndrome. In both cases, they're doubting themselves because they don't trust their audience. They fear ridicule, consequences, punishment.

If that sounds like you, here's my advice: Let them decide. Don't make the decision for your audience ahead of time, because you never know what's going to inspire or instruct someone else. So what if that imposter syndrome part of you is absolutely right and everyone *has* already heard the idea you're sharing? Here's something I've also heard again and again from the audience side: It's not just new ideas that people value hearing. They often need reminders of concepts they've forgotten or fresh takes on familiar ideas. How many books about baking bread does the world need? How many movies have been made about being yourself instead of trying to please others? Sometimes good ideas get so wrapped in cliché that the meaning just bounces off us until someone like you articulates it in a new way. You never know how your words might help someone. The French author André Gide has a snarky take on this that I've always found comforting: "Everything that needs to be said has already been said. But since no one was listening, everything must be said again."[6]

TRUST BOOSTERS

Trust is hard to come by. One of the first lessons of growing up is to stop trusting—don't trust strangers; don't take the internet's word for it; get a second opinion. Trust is a risk. So, why risk it? Because trust is the foundation of meaningful connections and the key to unlocking their potential.

Whether you're an individual, a team, or a leader, you want to make the most of your resources. Who wants to get only part of what they're paying for? If you inspire trust, people will bring their full talent, effort, and passion—resources that often go untapped without trust. If you're looking to support a healthy, trusting community that improves people's physical and mental health, as well as their personal and professional productivity, here are a few steps to make it happen.

STOP, LOOK, AND LISTEN

The first step in everything from mindfulness to preventative medicine is to pay attention. To gauge your community's health, start by paying attention: Do people trust that the others genuinely care for them? Is vulnerability rewarded or punished? Do relationships feel driven by love or fear?

CLARIFY

Articulate the type of community you want so that everyone understands what behavior is expected and why it will benefit them. Skeptics may scoff at prioritizing "soft" emotions, but research shows that positive connections enhance performance, resilience, and competitiveness.

PRIORITIZE

Don't let the urgent eclipse the important. Fires will always need putting out, but a strong leader builds practices that prevent and prepare for future conflagrations. Supporting a culture of trust takes more than an occasional team-building event. It requires involvement from all levels, especially leadership. When leaders model vulnerability and invest in relationships, it sends a powerful message about what matters to the community.

GIVE AND TAKE

"Although it may seem counterintuitive to assist others when you are feeling lonely," Dr. Murthy said, "giving and receiving help freely is one of the most tangible ways we experience our connections with each other."[7] Reciprocity is the key: Some are better at giving, others at taking, but both are necessary to build trust. Accepting help is as much a gift as giving it, but no one wants to be that person who only shows up when they want something. It's the balance that breathes trust into a community.

WELCOME THE FULL STORY

Authentic connections flourish when people feel safe to trust others with their full selves. Although 82 percent of employees want their organizations to see them as more than their job title, only 45 percent of employees feel that way.[8] Making space as a community to get to know the people behind the résumés—their stories, motivations, joys, and fears—will foster deeper connections among everyone. But that space won't just happen. It must be intentionally nurtured and protected. By you.

Whether it's your workplace or your writing group, community is about quality, not quantity. You can be plenty lonely even when you're surrounded by people or swamped with friend requests. You can also be perfectly nourished with just a few close connections. It's not about how many but about how meaningful.

FREE TO ALL, NOT A FREE-FOR-ALL

Community is more than proximity. It's about finding common ground without robbing anyone of their voice. This allows for diversity to thrive, but encouraging everyone to share their views can sometimes lead to conflict. That's why my activities emphasize not just speaking up but also listening up, showing up, and...erm...empathizing up.

When people know each other better as people and trust each other's motives, disagreement becomes a collision of priorities rather than a conflict between people. If people see value in each other, even though they disagree, they are primed to find the common ground that leads to productive compromise.

TRUSTING PLAY

Trust isn't a light switch. My activities are not a quick fix. You can't do one and say, "Yes! Now we're 17.8 percent more trusting!" These activities are an opportunity to nourish a perspective rather than achieve a measurable objective. Trust is a practice. Like playing an instrument, reading a crowd, or cooking from scratch, it takes time and effort to build intuitive understanding, and although you may not see immediate results, over time the growth is an exponential game changer.

Whether you choose to use these activities at a company offsite, game night with friends, or the family reunion, it's less about the artifact generated at the end of the activity and more about building understanding, sharing vulnerability, and practicing both trusting and being trustworthy. It's just a taste of what's possible, like a sample spoon of ice cream to whet your appetite for trust and make you hungry for more.

Different elements go into building and fueling trust. Activities like Blobviously (see page 201), Emblemottos (see page 147), and First Kiss Cocktail (see page 214) hit on different levels with different intensity, but they are all designed to give a sampling of trust with the hope that—like a mouthful of mint chip—people will be hooked once they know how delicious it tastes. Safe danger can soften the risks of seeing and being seen so that you can nourish honest, authentic connections built on trust. Activities like Homegrown Heroes (see page 93), I Contact (see page 225), and Towering Inspiration (see page 249) can help build a practice of looking deeper and appreciating the complexity and nuances of the people in our lives. These activities are not necessarily about building bonds between specific people but about teaching what it feels like to be "in trust" with someone else.

We're a bundle of contradictions. We believe we are unique ("Nobody really gets what I'm going through"). We also believe everyone is like us ("Nobody really likes kale"). Both beliefs occupy the same space at once. And both are true. The way to bring people together is to celebrate *both* what they have in common and what makes them unique. Activities like Blobviously (see page 201), Homemade Homage (see page 221), and Super Secret (see page 16) are designed to build community by highlighting both the commonalities and the diversity of its members.

A culture built on comparison and competition quickly narrows options to the right way or disaster. That's why it's so important to have other perspectives and expectations to get curious about, and the permission to express that curiosity. A community founded in trust resists tunnel vision and opens whole new landscapes of possibility.

> ## HABIT BUILDER
>
> ### Thank-You Notes
>
> I once got an email from a former colleague about a brief elevator conversation we'd had. I didn't even remember it, but something I said had helped him through a tough time. I was so touched. It made me think of what I appreciate about some of my favorite people and how they might not know how I felt, so I started making a habit of telling them.
>
> What if, today, you sent a quick email, text, or (gasp) handwritten letter letting someone know about a quality of theirs that made an impression on you? Remember how Aya was always so smiley and cheerful, even on Mondays? Let her know how much you appreciated that little boost of good energy. Remember how Trevor was always so willing to make time for you even when he was swamped? Let him know how you appreciated being valued that way.
>
> My wife liked this idea so much that for a milestone birthday, she wrote one heartfelt letter a week to fifty-two people who had made an impression on the shape of her life. But you don't have to do that. A two-minute text is enough. It's easy and kind; it's a great way to make sure people feel recognized for the small things they add to the world; and it's a great way for you to recognize how many great people you have in your life.

CHAPTER TEN

TO PREPARE FOR THE UNKNOWN, INSPIRE CREATIVITY

THE UNKNOWN

When I was a kid, one of my grandfather's favorite quotes was Louis Pasteur's: "Luck favors the prepared mind." Show up and do the work today, Grandpa explained, so if the magic happens tomorrow, you'll be sharp enough to recognize it.

If the magic happens tomorrow. That's the whole thing about tomorrow—you never know what it's got planned. The qualities covered in previous chapters don't guarantee inspiration or opportunities or happiness. But they'll prepare you. *If* inspiration strikes, *if* opportunity knocks, *if* the sun breaks through the clouds, you'll be ready to act without missing a step. You can't plan for the breeze, but you can open your windows wide. Conversely, *if* tomorrow shows up with something less than magical, you'll be ready for that too. This chapter focuses on how cultivating creativity can prepare you for whatever tomorrow has in store.

THE UNKNOWN UNKNOWN

And the way you prepare for the unknown? Most people start with what's likely and plan for that, which makes sense—sunblock will probably be more useful than snowshoes in Hawaii. But planning for the likely isn't the same as preparing for the unknown. The difference between planning and preparing comes down to what you don't know that you don't know:

What you know: The forecast says 50 percent chance of showers.

What you know you don't know: If it will rain.

What you don't know that you don't know: Hail the size of golf balls will demolish your umbrella.

You can *plan* for the first two, but the last will test how well you're *prepared* for real-time adaptation and problem-solving. I'm not saying don't plan. Obviously, stash three gallons of water per person in case of emergency and always buckle up. But to be ready for the unknown, you need to prepare—and that means cultivating creativity.

At its heart, creativity is all about dealing with the unknown. Instead of succumbing to the paralysis of indecision, creative minds embrace ambiguity as a catalyst for exploration, experimentation, and growth. The mental and emotional muscles creativity develops—adaptability, problem-solving, openness to new possibilities—are exactly what you need if something pops up out of the blue and you must pivot quickly, seize opportunities, or navigate complexity. Businesses that prioritize creativity are positioned to lead the way in their industries because they harness the collective intelligence and ingenuity of their teams to stay ahead of the curve and anticipate future trends.

When you get creative, you're not just training your brain—you are physically making it more flexible, adaptable, and resilient. Studies show that creativity drives the brain to form new behavioral connections and to grow

"Come on, there's got to be <u>something</u> for this in the company handbook!"

new synapses, directly increasing its plasticity—the ability to adapt to new experiences.[1] Researchers believe these changes result in a brain that is better prepared to acquire a wide range of skills, including STEM skills that usually (mistakenly) get positioned as the opposite of creativity.

When we think we're being productive by pushing creativity to the side and getting down to business, we're actually doing that business a great disservice. Creativity is the fastest way to develop the traits to help you zig when others zag, find unexpected solutions to unexpected obstacles, and play leapfrog instead of catch-up.

CULTIVATING CREATIVITY

Like grass poking through cracked sidewalk, creativity can flourish in unlikely places. Sometimes the worst circumstances ignite the fiercest creativity. But why complicate things? If you want to invite creativity into your world, cultivate the building blocks it needs to thrive.

CREATIVITY NEEDS PERMISSION

If you're feeding an atmosphere of fear and judgment, don't expect a whole lot of creativity. Creativity needs permission to make mistakes, make a problem, make a mess without looking over its shoulder. It needs freedom to play. That doesn't mean living with the mistakes, problems, and mess forever—just giving the process space and time to explore without worry.

Whether you're giving permission to yourself or your department, you can best respect and foster creativity by setting aside time and resources for it. Block space on the calendar. Allocate budget. Because if you want to know what really matters to people, look to the clock and the wallet. Everything else is ultimately just pretty words and empty intentions.

"Now go wild and build some bold, crazy stuff, and remember that the failing projects will be rewarded with a generous severance package."

CREATIVITY NEEDS FUEL

Imagine a new color. A color no one has ever seen before. You can't. The closest you can get is imagining that you can imagine it. As I mentioned earlier, our brains don't move that way. They don't create out of nothing. They can bend, blend, and break other ideas to make unheard-of new configurations. But something from nothing, they cannot do.

So you need to feed it. And what do you feed it? The world.

That's not very helpful, I realize, but that's what you feed it. Creativity feasts on sights, sounds, smells, ideas, news, art, arguments, giraffes, coffee, vendettas, landscapes, playgrounds, and face cream. All of it. You just never know ahead of time what it's in the mood for.

What's more helpful than *what* to feed it is *how*. You feed it by paying attention and being curious; by activating the explore mindset you had as a child. When you walk, pay attention to smells in the morning air. When you eat, pause to imagine how someone invented bread. When you argue, notice the patterns in how the conflict escalates. Collect the nuances of the world and your creativity will know what to do with it.

CREATIVITY NEEDS SAFE DANGER

To find its wings, creativity needs both a safe haven to build up its strength and a good shove to get it out of the nest. Creativity needs safety so joy can make it productive and energizing, but it also needs the danger of vulnerability to ground it in meaning and purpose. It needs optimism to keep moving when the path is unclear and the danger of curiosity to find new directions to explore. Creativity needs trust so you can gather the right people to share it with, people who can then push you out of your comfort zone. The nice thing is that this is a virtuous circle: Creativity builds the very qualities it depends on, growing stronger every time.

WHY NOT GIVE IT A TRY?

Another of my grandfather's sayings was, "It takes years to get rich overnight." If success really is 99 percent perspiration and 1 percent inspiration, why not make all that effort fun? Why not infuse it with creativity, joy, and imagination?

Because it wastes time. Because it's unnecessary. Because I'm not a child. Because I've got more important things to do. Those are the objections that come fast and ready.

From what I've seen, though, it's the opposite. So here are my responses:

- *It wastes time.* Starting with play can help you go faster and farther later, making the very most of your time.
- *It's unnecessary.* Fresh ideas need something to sweep away the cobwebs of habit, and play, fun, and creativity are the perfect tools for that necessary first step.
- *I'm not a child.* Children's brains are better wired than adults' to explore, absorb, and understand. This is something to be envied, not disparaged.
- *I've got more important things to do.* You may very well have other things to do. Whether those things are more or less important really depends on what you want from yourself.

Need proof your brain craves creativity? Look at any scrap of paper after a boring call. Doodles no doubt. Shapes, patterns, people, and the like. Or think of fidget spinners and mindless mobile apps—outlets for unused mental energy. You may not have even noticed all the ways your creative drive gets repressed by expectations, environments, and adulthood, but when your guard is down, it slips its bonds and leaps into the world. Maybe it's in how you arrange your desk, decorate your home, do your hair, host a party, or plant your garden. But it's there, waiting for its moment. It's like electricity. It's always around us, but for most of our history we ignored or feared it. Then we finally developed the tools to harness it. And it changed our entire world.

> *Don't tell yourself you're not creative.* Fine, maybe you're not getting a solo show at MoMA or selling out Wembley Stadium, but you are 100 percent creative enough to try the activities in this book. *Don't tell yourself you're already creative enough.* Creativity thrives on new experiences and unexpected inspiration. *Don't tell yourself you don't have time to be creative.* Try a habit builder while you're doing

something you have to do anyway such as commuting, the dishes, or waiting in line.

Ironically, many people have cloaked themselves in a sense of adulthood they constructed as children. It's a vision that was built from the outside looking in, looking at the outer shell instead of the inner experience. But now that we're all grown up, we get to choose what adulthood can really mean. We get to decide if it's worth risking that inherited, fabricated facade of adulthood in order to find something meaningful. Might it go badly? Sure. Might it go brilliantly? Sure. Is there any way to know ahead of time? Nope. In which case, we're faced with the most annoying question of all: What's the bigger risk: jeopardizing that old sense of self or keeping it safe?

SAFETY IS DANGER

They say the number one regret that people have when they look back over their life is that they didn't value the right things. Now, I recognize that it's easier for some retiree basking on a beach to say, "I shouldn't have worked so hard," than it is for someone midcareer who is trying to make rent or send the kids to camp. But reordering your priorities doesn't mean rejecting everything that's keeping you fed and sheltered. It just means rethinking how, when, and why you deploy your energy and talents.

John J. Walsh IV, author and cofounder of the design firm Iron Creative Communications, says he finds it helpful to think of regrets in two flavors: positive regrets and negative regrets. Positive regrets are for the risks you took. The times you put yourself out there and flopped. Negative regrets are the opposite. The times you didn't take the chance, order the thing from the menu, talk to the person who caught your eye. When you played it safe and missed out. "In a funny way," he says, "I don't regret my positive regrets. Even if they didn't work out the way I'd hoped, I didn't let fear make my choices for me."

I know that risking loss, failure, and judgment isn't something most of us wake up jonesing for. But if you're one of us who wants to hone your authentic, unique role in the world, if you're hungry for more inspiring experiences, excitement, and discovery, if your hope is to do groundbreaking work and make a difference, if you would love to enjoy deeper and more meaningful relationships, I can only say that, from what I've seen, taking those risks doesn't jeopardize your chances—it's actually the very best chance you've got.

Letting go of what's worked so far can feel impossible. I meet many successful people who feel stuck because the behaviors that made them successful come at a cost they don't want to pay anymore; however, they also don't want anything to change. It's been called the golden handcuffs—circumstances too good to walk away from even though you'd rather be anywhere else. But after too many nose-meeting-grindstone moments, many of us feel creeping awareness that the pace, the intensity, the codependency, the self-doubt, the perfectionism—the whatever—isn't compatible with happiness. And that is no longer a compromise we're happy with.

That recognition is only the starting gun. The stone in the shoe. Getting the shoe off and the stone out is a whole different game. It's tough because those traits that we've decided don't serve us, still, well, feel like *us*. They've been how we define ourselves for most of our adult lives. "I'm a perfectionist." "I'm a caretaker." "I'm no-nonsense." For many of us, these are traits we took on so early we can't remember a time without them. They were patterns and behaviors and mindsets that got us through tough times, hard challenges, helped us succeed where others stumbled. They became our armor against the pointy parts of life. Shedding that armor so you can grow beyond its limits is painful because the parts it was protecting need to bang against the world and bear the full glare of the sun for the first time.

Whether you call it disruption, disequilibrium, or discomfort, the message is clear: The biggest danger to your growth is safety. Not all flavors of safety. Just the ones smuggling stagnation in under their coat. If you want to move forward, you need to release your grip and reach forward for the next ring. That's not easy. It's not comfortable. It's not a guarantee. But it is the way forward.

Find your voice and unleash it. Pinpoint your uniqueness, use your sense of purpose to guide you in what to do with that uniqueness, and then put something into the world that matters.

We need it.

HABIT BUILDER

Wise Whys

One great technique for undoing the knotted threads of thought we all carry and spotlighting the dynamics at work beneath our beliefs and motivations is called Five Whys. The name pretty much says it all. You tap into your inner relentless three-year-old and keep asking why, each time a level deeper, letting your curiosity take over. Here's a silly example:

My nine-year-old is useless in the kitchen.

Why?

Because I haven't taught her to use the knives.

Why?

Because I'm afraid she'll cut off her fingers.

Why?

Because I cut myself badly as a kid.

Why?

Because I didn't know what I was doing.

Why?

Well, gee, because my parents didn't teach me how to use knives.

Playing Five Whys can be a very revealing way to better understand choices, disagreements, and habits or surface insights you might otherwise have overlooked.

You can also use it on yourself. If your goal is to improve how you show up in the world, it's super helpful to understand why you've been showing up the way you have until now. Each morning this week when you're brushing your teeth, look at yourself in the mirror and ask: "Do I like what I do, and do I like where I am doing it?" If the answers are yes, great. If the answers are consistently no, then probe with five levels of "why?" and explore your options.

PART III

MORE ACTIVITIES OF SAFE DANGER

CHAPTER ELEVEN

FACILITATION

WHY TRY?

"I've read your book. Isn't that enough? Why do I have to do the activities?"

Well, that's exactly why. If you have to ask, then you haven't done them. When my family was house hunting, the realtor gave us directions to an apartment: Get off at Clinton Washington, two lefts, straight past the oak that looks like a hamster, third on the left. It took us three wrong turns to find it. But it was a lovely apartment. When we went to take a second look, we found our way back much more easily. After we moved in, we could get back without even thinking about it. Creativity isn't learned, it's practiced. You need to walk its streets and learn your way around so that navigating it becomes second nature and you can always find your way back to where you want to live. Doing these activities is how you build that familiarity. When you live somewhere, you learn how to connect that place to all the other places you need to go. Doing these deceptively simple, admittedly silly activities is how you connect creativity to the areas of your life that could use a fresh boost of connection, inspiration, and purpose.

FACILITATION

Facilitating these activities in a way that gets everyone, introverts and extroverts, skeptics and converts, party kids and sticks-in-the-mud, to all show up and dig in can be tricky. You want to be joyful without being a clown. You want to open space for everyone without losing momentum. You want to be a center of gravity without making it all about you. Tricky. So I want to offer a few last pieces of advice I've picked up along the way as you begin to facilitate these in real time.

STAND TALL

This may feel obvious and natural to some, and utterly foreign and impossible to others, so I'll just put it out there: You want your audience to trust that they are in good hands, that you know what you're doing, that this will be worth their time. But no one will trust you if it looks like you don't trust yourself.

The key phrase here is *looks like*.

I noticed something over the years of sitting in audiences. To a startling degree, the quality of the content is less important than the quality of the delivery. When a speaker mumbles, apologizes, repeatedly talks about how nervous they are, it puts the audience in a position of judging them, of deciding whether to give them a break or give up on them. When someone speaks with confidence, however, the audience has been trained over the years to tacitly give them the benefit of the doubt—regardless of whether their message actually deserves it. We've all seen (too, too, too many) politicians deliver utterly meaningless statements with glowing confidence and the crowds will cheer. Because the interesting thing is that I, the audience member, have no idea what's going on behind their eyes. Whether they actually believe in themselves or their message or the intellect of their audience almost doesn't even matter. It's like a gift. The very same item will make a very different impression if it's beautifully wrapped in colorful ribbons and bows as opposed to if it's handed over in a grease-stained grocery bag. The difference between skepticism and enthusiasm is all about the presentation.

Speaking in public seems to be one of humanity's great terrors, to be avoided at all costs, along with spiders and foreign films. Which is natural.

Standing alone, surrounded by devouring eyes can't help but trigger a primal fear of being surrounded by salivating wolves waiting for an opening to strike and rip you to shreds. Well, at least it does for me. But I have a trick. I pretend to be my five-year-old kid, Quinn.

When I first started at IDEO, I was tapped to cohost a group of one hundred international IDEO enthusiasts who were coming to get some insight into our methods of human-centered research and rapid prototyping.[1] The plan was to give them a playful design challenge (neatly retrieve pushpins from a container without stabbing yourself), give them some playful materials (pipe cleaners, Legos, Play-Doh), and have them iterate a few times on the basis of research and feedback. To add a fun twist, my colleagues asked if I would bring Quinn in to be the pretend client the group would design for.

When we walked into the huge conference room, I noticed something I've never forgotten. Whereas I've always walked into a room of strangers and felt that wolf pack of eyes on me, like I needed to justify my presence and prove my value, Quinn walked in with a completely different attitude, something akin to, "Here I am, you lucky people!" And the audience played along, clearly feeling like they were in good, albeit small, hands with Quinn.

Now, Quinn has not been five years old since 2014. But from that day on, whenever I have to present to a crowd, I channel that five-year-old and walk in with that attitude of assurance that I belong up there in front. Over the years it's finally become second nature, but I also know that first nature is still lurking in there somewhere.

Every actor I know admits to opening-night nerves. But they go on with confidence. They do what they need to do to prepare and then they put on a show. This doesn't mean you should bury your feelings or lie to yourself. It means that if you need to rehearse to feel confident, then rehearse. If you feel better admitting your nerves, then admit them—then move on. But whatever you do, convene with conviction.

MODEL THE MODE

When I'm asking people to dip a toe in the vulnerability pool, I always take a lap first to show them (1) what's expected of them, and (2) that it's safe.

For example, if I'm asking them to share the story behind the music they loved at thirteen years old, I say something like, "Well, I pretended to like Led Zeppelin because that was the favorite band of the coolest kid in our group. But I really liked mopey, angry music in that stage—Depeche Mode, The Smiths, The Doors, Nine Inch Nails—because I was sad and found that being angry made that sadness hurt less. I wasted many of my teenaged years defining myself by criticizing things that were different from the narrow persona I'd cultivated rather than expanding the possibilities of who I might be." Or in an exercise about optimism, I might acknowledge that I have clinical depression, so it's always hard for me to protect that flame of hope in the face of what may go wrong. Whatever the topic, I always try to offer up something that is personal—but not overly personal...I don't want them to feel burdened or horrified. It's meant as a welcome. Like the decor in a restaurant: it's meant to set the mood and clarify the mode of their engagement.

SHARE THE STRUCTURE

Although I like to maintain an element of surprise and spontaneity, I always give the audience or my clients the plan at the start. There's a mantra about the three steps of a presentation that I borrow from when I'm facilitating:

1. Tell them what you're going to tell them.
2. Tell them.
3. Tell them what you've told them.

In action that looks something like, "Okay, so without going into too much detail yet, basically today you're going to be sharing some stories with each other, making something out of those stories, and then talking about what you made." It can be that simple. But it gives people a basic map of what to expect and that lets their amygdala calm down. Otherwise, there's always a part of them preparing for the unexpected.

Then after they do the activity, and after I've shared the why (discussed later in this chapter), I play back for them not the mechanics of the event but the emotional elements they were engaged in. It can be as simple as "I hope you all enjoyed getting to fail joyfully, getting to find success in failure, and hearing and sharing some of the stories that have made you who you are." But this closes the loop on the safety that we opened with and lets them know that we have indeed delivered on what we promised at the start.

EJECT BUTTON

One of the most important elements of inviting people into safe danger is offering them a way out. I think of it like an eject button. The more I ask of people, the bigger I make that button, because I want to reassure them that this is their choice.

For example, with Super Secret (see page 16) I'm asking people to share personal stories, and this can obviously tread into very personal territory. To make this feel less intrusive, I make it clear that for our purposes the definition of *secret* is pretty broad. No PIN codes or passwords. Just something that the other people in the room won't know. If you want to share that you were a foster kid, that's lovely. But if the most personal you're comfortable with is that you're super fast on the remote, that will also work for the activity. I never want to humiliate anyone by excluding them. So rather than making it an all-or-nothing choice, I try to build in levels of participation so people who would normally run for the hills can at least remain in the room and not be singled out.

At the same time, I do also try to frame the eject button in a gently discouraging way. For Super Secret, I'll acknowledge that everyone has a line between what's comfortable to share and what's too personal. I'm clear that I'm not asking them to cross that line. But I do encourage them to consider whether that line is in the right place. Might they move it a bit? Push it a bit? In Homegrown Heroes (see page 93), I'm clear that they are in control of how vulnerable their share is, but I also tell them that what I've seen time and again is that the people who get the most vulnerable are the most inspirational to others. So I move the spotlight off them and make it less about their vulnerability and more about their generosity. With Moving Stories (see page 31), I give people the opportunity to opt out of the dancing portion, but I do ask them to consider what is holding them back. If these circumstances aren't safe enough, when they've been given permission, when everyone else is being equally ridiculous, when no one will judge them, what would need to be true for them to participate? Would *anything* be enough to allow them to let themselves let loose? This way, even if people are going to use the eject button, it's an opportunity for reflection. Even declining the activity has value.

Counterintuitively, I've actually found that the bigger the escape button, the less inclined people are to use it. Plus, the activities have more impact when people felt they've chosen to participate rather than been forced.

KINDNESS OVER KIDDING

One of the hardest lines to walk is the one between authenticity and leadership. I'm a naturally sarcastic person. Playfully teasing banter has been my primary mode of discourse since middle school. But I've learned from experience that I can't bring that into the room. I never tease a participant. Even if they start it. I never use anything they've offered against them. If they've mentioned a love of coffee and are slow to respond, I never offer them an espresso to perk them up. Playful banter is fun, but it also puts people on guard. It may be a joyful guard, but it's still a guard. I've watched the shutters close behind someone's smiling eyes and realized too late that I'd crossed a line.

NO COMPARISONS

There's always one. Someone always jokingly promises to blow the others away or admits defeat from the beginning. There's a pervasive compulsion to compete. I try to shut that down as quickly and gently as possible. It's one of the few areas that I'm pretty merciless about. There's no room here for comparison. Connection, correlation, parallels, yes. But no hierarchy. We often use kindergarten materials in our activities for just that reason. We want to put everyone back into that macaroni-necklace mindset of just creating something for the joy of creating it. No looking over their shoulder to see whether they need to course correct to match the group, no judging or comparing. This moment is about supporting each other, finding common ground, learning from each other. If everyone is focused on where they fit in, then they're making it all about the context of this moment—being the best or the worst in this particular group. We want them thinking bigger and broader than that. We want them creating from their authentic, timeless self. If people are busy protecting themselves from judgment (by defeating their competitors, by taking the sting out of failure through self-deprecation), then they're focusing on the wrong thing.

LEAD WITH CURIOSITY

When people present their work, they tend to focus on the finished product and how it came out. They tend to expect judgment—is it good, bad, success, disaster, did they do it right, did they embarrass themselves? Critiques are important to quality work. No doubt. There's a time and a place for critiques. This isn't it. This is early in the process, this is raw, this is when things are opening up, so we leave the critique tools alone. Instead of focusing on the results, I focus on the choices that led there. "I see you've chosen to work in all different shades of blue. I'd love to hear about that choice." "In the middle of your song you've got a moment that gets really quiet. Tell us more about that." I focus on the choices because that's the aspect most aligned with their intentions. Regardless of how it came out, what were they trying to achieve? That's the heart of our work here. What was their motivation? What do they want to convey? "You've got this interesting peephole here that both focuses and limits someone's viewpoint. Can you share your thinking behind that?"

This applies beyond facilitation. I learned that long ago from my kids' art teacher. If I say their drawing is great, then I've locked them in a standard of beauty. They start repeating what they've done in hopes of earning more praise. They become afraid of trying new things if those won't be praised to the same degree. But if I say, "Ooooh, tell me about all these details you've added to the whale's top hat," then I'm offering recognition without judgment.

CONVERSATIONS INSTEAD OF COMPLIMENTS

One of the hardest things for me to do when facilitating is resist the urge to praise quality. When someone creates something that really knocks my socks off, my instinct is to say so—to say, "Wow! That's incredible! It's so beautiful / insightful / clever / smart." But what I've found is that this sort of praise does two things that I don't want. First, it shuts down the conversation. Maybe the person feels proud and that the work speaks for itself, or they feel they got lucky and don't know how to react, or they feel humble and are wary of going on and on about themselves. Either way, the conversation is always richer when I'm more curious than complimentary.

The second thing it does is set off a barrage of comparisons in everyone else's head. "Is mine as beautiful?" "Mine is better than that one!" "Mine isn't as good, so how can I follow that?" Again it closes off the openness of the conversation. We don't want anyone to be keeping track in their heads of who is more loved than anyone else. We don't want anyone to feel less than or that they need to prove they are more than. Leading with curiosity instead of judgment allows everyone to feel equally valued, equally seen, equally loved.

As hard as it is to hold back the compliments, holding back consolation is even harder. And even more important. When someone shares that they're struggling with something, I don't say, "That's awful." Instead I ask something like, "How are you handling that?" It's not my place to validate, judge, or assess, because the moment I do that (1) everyone else in the group begins hierarchizing their own issues, and (2) it becomes about how I am reacting (as the voice of authority) as opposed to what they are sharing. I want the spotlight to stay on them, and I want everyone to feel seen and equally entitled to that spotlight.

When you focus on the choices people make rather than the results of those choices, you connect about the process, the thinking, the intention. And those are all tools that they're going to use in the future. This particular activity is going to end in minutes. Whether it's a success or a failure doesn't matter in the long term. What matters for the next one and the next one and the one after that is the mindset they bring. So, that's what I focus on.

DON'T BE SHY ABOUT THEIR WHY

These activities are designed to get people sharing more than they may have expected to share. It can be a very vulnerable moment. Respect their efforts by meeting it with curiosity. Rather than just nodding, ask one or two thoughtful, nonjudgmental follow-up questions that explore their choices or dig a little deeper in their thought process. Open-ended questions give them a safe path and an invitation to share juuuust a bit more. Try to unearth the why, the feelings beneath the facts. For example, "Why did you choose this motto *now*?" or "What was it about that music that spoke to you?" or "What's going to be your biggest obstacle in making this happen?" You're not being nosy; you're just trying to gently encourage them to offer a peek into the values and priorities that define them.

CLOSE WITH YOUR WHY

I always like to close by revealing the details of what the activity was about and why certain choices were made. This is because much of what happens during the activity—the vulnerability, the generosity, the inspiration, the connection—is experiential and intuitive. Participants may not even have noticed what was going on behind the mental scenes. So I point it out and give them the vocabulary to articulate all the elements they've just experienced. That can go a long way to both justifying the experience in their eyes and giving them the words with which to spread the message of what they're taking away.

CHAPTER TWELVE

THE ACTIVITIES

Blobviously 201
Childhood Hoodwinks 204
Chroma Aroma 206
Conceptual Candies 208
Delightful Doppelgängers 210
Expert-Tease 212
First Kiss Cocktail 214
Fort Disruption 217
Head in the Game 219
Homemade Homage 221
Hour Gift to You 223
I Contact 225
Infantile Inspiration 227
Karaoke Cruelty 229
Kinda Kintsugi 231

Kindness Rocks 233

Masking the Darkness 235

Memory Floss 237

Mind Maps... 239

Orchestra of Optimism 241

Poetic Powers 243

Sew Many Rules 245

Slow Down to Speed Up 247

Towering Inspiration 249

Twinsies 252

BLOBVIOUSLY: SEEING THROUGH NEW EYES

Primary Quality
Curiosity

Supporting Themes
Valuing Diverse Perspectives
Community Bonding
Relaxing Perfectionism

THE WHAT

Remember in first grade after the art lesson when everyone folded their paint-filled wax paper in half to make beautiful butterfly blobs? Never mind the blank-eyed self-portraits, *these* were the things we were excited about and wanted to show off. There was a bit of magic to them, because they couldn't be controlled. Mixing that memory with a certain famous psychological tool got us to Blobviously (with apologies to Ms. Karpinski and Dr. Hermann Rorschach). Say what you see.

THE HOW

Create: Everyone begins by globbing, gooping, or dribbling paint on a sheet of card stock (I've always used black paint on white paper to keep it simple, but you do you), folding it in half, and smoothing it flat to create an abstract shape inside.

Interpret: Lay these blobs, swirls, whorls out on a table with a couple of blank index cards underneath each sheet. Everyone moves to an image created by someone else, takes a minute to absorb it, and then, beginning with the phrase, "Obviously I see..." they use one of the index cards to write down what they see in the squiggles, blotches, and blots. An alien having a picnic? A child at the beach? Two frogs kissing? There's no wrong answer. After five minutes, everyone turns their card over so it can't be read and slips it back under the image. Then they move to a different image and take another few minutes to absorb and interpret that one.

Share Back: Once everyone has interpreted four different blobs, they go back to the image they created and collect all the interpretations. Depending on the size of your group, you can have people read all four aloud or just pick the two most distinct.

A few examples of what I've gotten back from a single image:

"Obviously, I see two girls, next-door neighbors, leaping off their roofs, ponytails flying into the air. They laugh and touch hands midfall—pattycake in the sky. They live in that moment. They haven't given a thought to the next."

"Obviously, I see war, smoke, clouds, and fire in the distance. Two figures running in opposite directions. Their steps are determined, but light and airy, almost like as soon as they exit the frame, they'll grow wings and fly."

"Obviously, I see two young seahorses (probably siblings) conspiring with each other. They're developing a secret plan because they each have a precious pearl but need to find a secret spot to stash them for safekeeping."

All different, yet all there in the image. In the end, each image has multiple stories—stories that say more about the viewer than the image itself. After everyone has shared, open the floor for comments, then close out by sharing the why.

THE WHY

There's a reason that collaboration has value. We all may see the same challenge, but we interpret it our own way. We can't help but see the world through the lens of our own history, biases, emotions, and experience. It's not that there's no right answer but that they're all equally right answers, depending on who's asked the question. Blobviously lets people practice sharing ideas without being influenced by the perspectives or judgment of others—trusting that their individual voice is as important as anyone else's.

When we let a single voice dominate a conversation or shame dissenters into silence, we collapse possibilities into a single option. This activity is a gentle but memorable reminder not to do that, not to assume that we all see the same problem or the same solutions. If we remember to push ourselves beyond what seems obvious at first glance, if we have the trust we need to risk an unconventional idea, we can enrich our perspectives and see things from multiple, unanticipated angles.

THE MATERIALS

Paper: I like card stock so that it doesn't bleed through but will still dry pretty quickly.

Paint: Acrylic, tempera, anything with enough viscosity to smoosh—so, no watercolors. Color is dealer's choice. Simple black creates simple silhouettes that leave most of the work to the imagination, but a nice set of colors make for a beautiful collection of evocative images. Your call.

Index Cards: I like lined cards to encourage people to fill the thing up with their descriptions, but again, anything can work.

CHILDHOOD HOODWINKS: QUESTIONING THE OBVIOUS

Primary Quality
Unconventional Thinking

Supporting Themes
Storytelling
Empathy
Humility

THE WHAT

A light, playful activity that draws on the misunderstandings we carried as children and asks people to imagine a world in which those misunderstandings were true.

THE HOW

Reflect: Everyone is asked to think back to something they misunderstood as a child. Ideally, each person comes up with three. Did you think all dogs were boys and all cats were girls? Did your mother tell you that the music meant the ice cream truck was out of ice cream? Did you try to get through the mirror to the other side?

Create: Imagining the misunderstanding was actually true, dream up a brochure for a product based on that misunderstanding. A trophy for the person who is "winning at traffic" in front of all the other cars. A welcome mat for the cottages where cottage cheese is made. A PSA to keep your wings to yourself when riding the Staten Island Fairy.

Share: Everyone takes turns sharing their creation and explaining the inspiration. Open the floor for comments, then close out by sharing the why.

THE WHY

This activity is a laugh-filled snapshot of the humble beginnings beneath our professional demeanor. Revisiting the silly ways we once saw the world is an excellent way to remind ourselves of all the assumptions we take for granted, the nuances and subtleties of language and culture, and all the ways that the world might be interpreted differently. It's also a joyful way to refresh the childlike eyes with which we once understood our lives and the world around us. Infusing our adult, professional life with that childlike energy and creative thought process can help us to reframe challenges, refuel purpose, and reimagine possibilities.

THE MATERIALS

Paper and multicolored markers

Nice-to-Haves: Scissors, glitter glue, card stock

CHROMA AROMA: SYNERGETIC SYNESTHESIA

Primary Quality
Questioning the Obvious

Supporting Themes
Empathy
Problem-Solving
Failure

THE WHAT

Asking people to visualize a smell is always going to be an exercise in futility because, well, smells aren't visual. This activity pushes you to explore the boundaries of smell and sight by trying and failing to make them do each other's job.

THE HOW

Create: Everyone chooses three selections from a large sampling of colorful, aromatic finger paints laced with spices, herbs, and essential oils. For each selection, they finger-paint the *experience* of smelling the scent—not a picture of the smell's source, but a picture of what it feels like for their body to encounter that particular smell. No pine trees for pine scents. Tell a visual story of the smell so that someone else will know what to expect to feel when they lean in to sample your scratch-and-sniff painting.

Name: Give the smell a new, original name based on your experience and paint this new name on the page as well.

Share: Hang up your aromatic art, have the group sample each other's vision, and facilitate a brief discussion after each. Do you agree with their interpretation? Does a whiff of "Froomy" smell like you expected? Does "Lahh" live up to its imagery? What about "Boooomba"? After everyone has had a turn, open the floor for comments, then close out by sharing the why.

THE WHY

Every new attempt to paint a smell will be a chance to spend time with failure, get familiar with frustration, and immerse yourself in the impossible. This is great training for when you want to take up another task that feels worthwhile but doesn't promise success.

Translating experiences between the senses requires breaking away from the mental shorthand that has served us all our lives. This is analogous to what we're asking of ourselves as we explore new ideas and territories: to give up the easy and familiar ways of thinking and stretch into a new frame of mind.

THE MATERIALS

Rainbow of finger paints (When you infuse the paints with the essential oils to mix up the senses and scents, put the pine in the red, the cinnamon in the blue, etc.)

Variety of brushes, cups of water for each person, paper, selection of essential oils, smocks or large trash bags people can wear as smocks, wet wipes (or easy access to soap and water)

CONCEPTUAL CANDIES: EDIBLE ASPIRATIONS

Primary Quality
New Angles on Old Ideas

Supporting Themes
Unconventional Thinking
Storytelling
Imagination

THE WHAT

Take ephemeral qualities or powers and transmute them into candy form. Willy Wonka was the king of metaphoric candies, and this is your chance to step into his colorful shoes.

THE HOW

Reflect: Start by giving your participants a prompt that touches on the outcome you're after. In the past I've used, "Think about the qualities or actions that would help your team excel in the year ahead," "Think about the help you needed when you were facing your biggest challenge," and "Think about the feelings you get when you're doing your favorite things."

Create: Now, imagine a magical candy that evokes, bestows, or enhances those qualities. Use crafting objects to create a toy version of that magical candy that will delight and surprise your team with the flavor of sweet success. Using shipping tags or index cards, create a label with the candy's name and tagline on one side and an explanation of what it does to you on the other.

Share: Everyone takes turns sharing their creation and explaining the inspiration. Open the floor for comments, then close out by sharing the why.

THE WHY

Allowing play to overlap with serious needs merges childhood delights with grown-up daydreams and opens the space for the imagination to run wild, unlock new solutions, and inspire new insights. There are always things people want to say to each other that can be tricky to articulate. "This candy helps everyone stay joyful at quarter end" is a playful way to point out that your colleagues become stressed-out monsters every three months. Translating emotional qualities like flexibility under pressure into physical ones like bendy straws or pipe cleaners is a way to give form and tone to an intention and anchor it in a metaphor that people can easily call back up when they need it.

THE MATERIALS

Pipe cleaners, pom-poms, googly eyes, markers, fabrics, felts, mirrors, gem stickers, beads, feathers, string, anything else within reach

Glue guns, scissors, colored shipping tags with strings

Packaging—I like using cellophane bags and tying them closed with the shipping tag labels, but I've also used plastic wrap or Ziplocs in a pinch

DELIGHTFUL DOPPELGÄNGERS: SINCERE FLATTERY

Primary Quality
Problem-Solving

Supporting Themes
Questioning the Obvious
Persistence
Tactile Thinking

THE WHAT

Make paper feel like not-paper. The challenge is straightforward: Use paper to re-create a very different, randomly selected texture. The experience is very much not straightforward. It requires lateral thinking, ingenuity, creativity, patience, and persistence. Plus, the guessing game is a fun group activity that leads to laughter and surprises.

THE HOW

Select: Everyone blindly picks from a basket of slips of paper, each of which names a different kind of texture—leather, sponge, spider web, hair, fish scales, velvet, orange peel, concrete, denim, sand, and the like. Keep this selection a secret—people will try to guess it later. (A fun alternative is to use feelings instead of texture. What does happy paper feel like as opposed to angry paper?)

Create: Everyone gets thirty minutes to make a regular sheet of paper feel like the texture they've selected. Anything they want to use to make this happen is fair game.

Share: Gather everyone back around. One by one, each creation is presented without a clue as to what it's supposed to be. Everyone touches the creation and tries to guess the texture. No prizes or winners, just fun. Open the floor for comments, then close out by sharing the why.

THE WHY

Though constraints are frustrating at first, they are often the key to sparking real invention. It's a great way to think more carefully about the nuances we take for granted and push our minds toward unconventional problem-solving.

THE MATERIALS

Paper, scissors, tape, whatever's in reach

EXPERT-TEASE: THE GIFT OF KNOWLEDGE

Primary Quality
Storytelling

Supporting Themes
Connection
Generosity
Diversity

THE WHAT

Taking a cue from medieval German house books (as one does), which asked guests to share their expertise with their hosts in the form of recipes, dances, alchemy, and so forth, this activity is all about sharing what you know. Tell me something I don't know.

THE HOW

Reflect: Think about the specialized wisdom you've acquired during your life—from finding feng shui to grooming a shar-pei. Anything is fair game.

Create: Pick a teachable aspect (less advice, more instruction) and create an illustrated, step-by-step how-to that shares your wisdom in a way that everyone can absorb and appreciate. Make your page as beautiful as it is insightful.

Share: Everyone takes turns sharing their page and explaining how they acquired this wisdom. Close out with the why.

THE WHY

This is an unexpected way of connecting a variety of personal experiences and expertise. It's an opportunity to take personal inventory, celebrate yourself and each other, and spend a little time thinking through the aspects of life we may take for granted. Plus, in the end, you've got a unique collection of knowledge to draw from.

THE MATERIALS

Paper or card stock, multicolored markers

Nice-to-Haves: Scissors, glitter glue, water colors, paint pens

FIRST KISS COCKTAIL: SIPPABLE STORIES

Primary Quality
Vulnerability

Supporting Themes
Storytelling
Problem-Solving
Community

THE WHAT

Tell a story with flavors. Translate a memory into a strange and unfriendly storytelling medium: taste.

THE HOW

Reflect: Everyone is asked to think back to their first kiss. (Meaningful, memorable, happy kisses only. Thanksgiving smooches from Aunt Rita don't count.) Take five minutes and have partners exchange stories to get people laughing and remembering. This is more than just the facts, it's the story—what was the context, the buildup, the location, the sights, sounds, smells? The aftermath.

Create: Everyone is given twenty minutes to craft and garnish a beverage that evokes that story of their first kiss. Maybe they want to lean into visuals like Artemis, who locked lips with a beachside lifeguard. She used blue curaçao for the blue ocean, a lemon wheel garnish for the sun, and a maraschino for the cherry lip balm she hastily applied right before (coconut rum for the smell of sunblock). Or maybe their story is better told through metaphor, like Gabrielle's. Gabrielle is French and shared a nervous *premier bisou* with an Italian exchange student. Her drink was a mixture of French Lillet and Italian Campari, all shaken up. Maybe they're more literal like Angel, who added a few drops of unpleasantly spicy hot sauce to a glass of tepid water for the blasé young lady who was a blasé kisser until the end—when she tried to up her game by biting his lip.

After creating your beverage, create a recipe card for it that features its name and ingredients and offers a summary of what emotions to expect from consuming the drink.

Share: Share the story of your kiss with the whole group and explain your liquid interpretation. Open the floor for comments, then close out with the why.

THE WHY

This activity is the epitome of what I mean by low stakes / highly personal. Your first kiss is a milestone of your personal history, a secret that rarely gets shared, yet it's distant enough that you can share all the cringeworthy details with a smile and laugh along with everyone else. There's no need to be embarrassed when everyone's story is equally embarrassing. Everyone walks away with a privileged peek into each other's history and feeling a bit more open and connected.

This is a favorite February activity for Valentine's Day, but it's also a fun twist for a happy hour or dinner party with friends. Just like any good beverage, there's a lot going on beneath the surface of this activity—emotional vulnerability, analogous thinking, and interpersonal connection.

THE MATERIALS

The ideal setup (I've never actually had all these at the same time, but it's a good starting list to choose from and add to):

Staple nonalcoholic beverages—seltzer, tonic, soda, juice
Staple alcoholic beverages—vodka, gin, tequila, whiskey, bourbon, scotch
Nonstaple beverages—crème de menthe, Gatorade, passionfruit juice, etc.
Odd selections—popcorn vodka, clamato juice, lavender syrup, etc.
Garnish staples—lemon, lime, cherries, olives, onions
Fun garnishes—chipotle salt, cocktail pickles, smoky salt
Childhood-themed things—gum, candy, chips, etc.
Glassware—martini, shot, rocks, tumbler, etc. More variety the better
Skewers or toothpicks for garnishes, cocktail umbrellas
Note cards or card stock and markers for the recipe cards

FORT DISRUPTION: INSPIRATION FROM IMPERMANENCE

Primary Quality
Fresh Eyes

Supporting Themes
Inspiration
Problem-Solving
Joy

THE WHAT

Protect yourself from a routine rut with a pillow fort. A remote gathering that gets everyone away from their screens.

THE HOW

Reassure: Open by explaining the why. This is a particularly childish activity and adults have an easier time playing when they understand the purpose.

Create: Sheets, blankets, holiday lights, and of course pillows are called to action as everyone takes twenty minutes to create a designated "happy place." Make it comfy and fun. Secret entrances are encouraged. Everyone must add at least one impractical, indulgent element to make the space as special, wild, and magical as possible.

Share: One by one, everyone plays real estate agent, showing off their creations. Ask everyone to work from their fort for the remainder of the day.

THE WHY

Many of us become overly acquainted with our homes, especially those who work from home (WFH). A pillow fort is an easy, unexpected, and playful way to breathe new life into the spaces we spend so much time in. By disrupting our everyday routine, it helps us reclaim a corner of our overinhabited spaces. This is an invitation to unleash reckless childlike curiosity by taking the pieces of the adult world (sheets, couches) and shift from asking, "What does this do?" to wondering, "What might this become?"

Because they are only temporary, pillow forts invite us to rethink our space without consequences. They can be a special happy place that doesn't need to be realistic or practical about tomorrow—it is all about joyfully satisfying the needs of the moment. These are creations of intention. They're inconvenient. They're impractical. But still. They're so worth it.

THE MATERIALS

Laptops or phones with video capabilities

Everything within reach

HEAD IN THE GAME: CREATING RULES AS CREATIVE TOOLS

Primary Quality
Problem-Solving

Supporting Themes
Joy
Collaboration
Storytelling

THE WHAT

Thirty minutes to invent a game. Ever notice the kids on a playground only need about thirty seconds to invent a game out of nowhere? Stack the pine cones. One-foot backward-hop races. A game is just rules and an objective. So let's make up some new ones.

THE HOW

Plan: Divide your group into cohorts of two to four people. Give them thirty minutes to invent a game. It must have an objective and a clear way to win or lose.

Create: Any objects in the home or office are fair game. I like to give them a constraint to give them somewhere to start, such as "you must use gravity." Or magnets. Or silence. Or eye contact. Or your hobbies.

Share: The teams explain the rules of their game and demonstrate how to play. When everyone has shared, close out briefly with the why and then let everyone loose to go play the games.

THE WHY

Most of us have been trained to learn the rules and follow them. This is a nice moment to take back control, create our own rules, and flex our imagination by conjuring fun out of nowhere.

THE MATERIALS

Pipe cleaners, pom-poms, googly eyes, markers, popsicle sticks, fabrics, felts, mirrors, gem stickers, beads, feathers, string, disposable coffee cups, air-dry clay, balloons, wooden blocks, anything else within reach

Glue guns, scissors, tape, markers

HOMEMADE HOMAGE: CREATIVITY WITHIN CONSTRAINTS

Primary Quality
Connection

Supporting Themes
Problem-Solving
Trust
Community

THE WHAT

Put yourself in your idol's shoes. This activity works with the music that spoke to people's hearts when they were coming of age. We have them re-create an iconic album from their past... with themselves as the star.

THE HOW

Reflect: Everyone thinks back to when they were fourteenish, at that pivotal moment of self-discovery and self-definition. Think about the album that meant the most to you at that phase of your life. What was the music that spoke to your heart, that brought you joy, got you through breakups and bus rides, and helped make your who you are? What is that album?

Create: Everyone has thirty minutes to re-create that album cover with themselves as the star. Ziggy Stardust face paint or just posing like a Joshua tree holding loofahs. Think about the composition, the color palette, the mood, the message. Kitchen utensils, toys, fruit, blankets, pets, brooms, shoes, Photoshop. Whatever works.

The facilitator should take note of the albums selected and play tracks from those selections while people work.

Share: If possible, place the creation next to an image of the original. Everyone shares their revised album and the stories of who they were when they listened to it, how they first heard it, and why it resonated with them. When everyone has shared, open the floor for comments, then close out with the why.

THE WHY

This is a great way to get to know colleagues and friends a layer deeper—not just by sharing music and imagery that mean something to them but in the way they talk about them and the story behind the meaning. It's an opportunity for the kind of low-stakes but highly personal sharing that builds community bonds.

It's also an opportunity to build creative problem-solving muscles. Considering an image closely enough to re-create it requires a slow, thoughtful moment to soak in the nuances and appreciate the details. Then imagination and creativity kick in as you have to make do and compensate for inferior materials. It forces you to extract the essence of an image you love and find a new way to communicate it.

THE MATERIALS

In-Person
  Anything you can find
  Laptop or phone to edit the picture together
  Nice-to-Have: Color printer to print them all out for the share

Online
  Collaborative slide deck or white board for everyone to work in

HOUR GIFT TO YOU: REFRESH HOW YOU REFRESH

Primary Quality
Connection

Supporting Themes
Inspiration
Generosity
Connection

THE WHAT
An hour of indulgent refueling…for someone else.

THE HOW

Commit: First, everyone opens their calendars and finds a free waking hour in the next week. Block it off.

Create: Everyone thinks of how they would best use that hour to recharge, rejuvenate, and refill their energetic well. Not just relax, but what refuels them when they're feeling low. Biking? Baudelaire? Beyoncé? Or perhaps simply coffee and cupcakes. They know themselves best.

Now they are going to give that hour to someone else. On a piece of paper, they will take this mystery recipient by the hand and guide them—where they go, what they do, what they pay attention to, and so forth. Take all the decisions off their shoulders and lead them along an hour of surprise, relaxation, observation, or whatever.

Swap: Everyone shares the hour they've crafted and explains why they find the elements in it so refreshing. Then they seal it in an envelope and draw some sort of image on it (so that they can tell it's theirs). When all the envelopes have been collected, everyone picks one at random (no taking your own). Over the next week, when people reach that hour they blocked off, they open their envelope, and take a surprising little detour from their day. Extra credit for snapping a selfie during the outing and sending it back to the group. Then, close out with the why.

THE WHY

This is a chance to mix up our routines and ensure that we make time to replenish our fuel. It's an opportunity to gift someone your most personal suggestion on self-care, while graciously receiving the same from someone else and getting to know them in a unique way by experiencing what fuels them.

It is an hour built on trust (putting ourselves in someone else's hands and trusting them to care for us), generosity (the feeling of excitement that comes when giving someone something meaningful), vulnerability (revealing our weak spots and how we tend to them), and curiosity (openness to try something new and unfamiliar).

THE MATERIALS

Paper (colored paper is more fun), pens (colored markers are more fun), envelopes

I CONTACT: WASHING THE WINDOWS OF THE SOUL

Primary Quality
Connection

Supporting Themes
Vulnerability
Empathy

THE WHAT

An emotional staring contest. In 2009, performance artist Marina Abramović sat in a chair at the Museum of Modern Art, and other people sat across from her. That was it. No talking, they just looked at each other. People lined up down the block to see the performance. It's a powerful thing to look someone in the eyes. This is my twist on the experience, a mash-up of Marina and third-grade staring contests.

THE HOW

Words: Everyone is paired up and given ten minutes to find the thing they have most in common and the thing they have least in common. Both raised by single mothers, but one is a night owl and the other is a morning lark. Both watched *The Wizard of Oz* last night, but one's happy place is the beach, the other the snowy mountains. Et cetera.

Eyes: All talking stops. Each pair sits knee to knee—no tables between them—and makes silent eye contact for four minutes. That's it. Sit silently. Hold eye contact. Listen with the eyes.

Hands: Each partner has twenty minutes to make a gift for the other celebrating their connection, bridging their distance, or just processing the experience. If you're in-person, this gift can be something tangible; if you're remote, you can create something using your digital toolbox. The gift is acknowledging that you heard the other, that the connection was flowing in both directions.

Share: Each pair takes turns giving their gift to their partner and explaining the thinking behind it. Open the floor for comments, then close out with the why.

THE WHY

This is an opportunity to strip away all the distractions and deflections and connect head-on with one another. We rarely take the time to look at another person deeply. We rarely allow ourselves to be openly stared at. In that silence, there are new opportunities for contemplation, curiosity, and insight about ourselves and our partners. Connecting so deliberately with another person can bring awkward giggles or welling tears. Where does the discomfort come from that makes us squirm and laugh and wish we could look away? People are so much more than the shorthand we use to think of them. This activity is a chance to feel that.

THE MATERIALS

In-Person: Glue guns, scissors, tape, markers, pipe cleaners, pom-poms, googly eyes, popsicle sticks, fabrics, felts, mirrors, gem stickers, beads, feathers, string, disposable coffee cups, air-dry clay, balloons, wooden blocks, anything else within reach

Online: Collaborative slide deck or white board, collection of about 100 beautiful images (from nature, from technology, from bodies, from faces, from history, from culture, from space, from animals, from architecture, from food)

INFANTILE INSPIRATION: MEMORIES MADE SNUGGLY

Primary Quality
Inspiration

Supporting Themes
Storytelling
Vulnerability
Generosity

THE WHAT

Gift someone a happy memory. This is an activity to celebrate someone being in a family way. It's a wonderful way to take inspiration from the stories that made us who we are.

THE HOW

Reflect: Pick one of your earliest, happiest memories.

Create: Use fabric paint to decorate a plain white onesie with an iconic image that represents that memory.

Share: Share the story behind your onesie's image and give your recipient this lineup of truly unique baby shower gifts. Close out by sharing the why.

THE WHY

It's always worthwhile to take stock of the things, people, and places that made us happy. Exchanging those stories with others is both a way to understand each other more deeply and open a window on the pieces that make us who we are. It's also a way to reconnect with the things that bring us joy and tap that well for future inspiration.

THE MATERIALS

Plain white cotton onesies (organic if you're feeling thoughtful), fabric paints

KARAOKE CRUELTY: PRESENTING UNDER PRESSURE

Primary Quality
Resilience

Supporting Themes
Creative Thinking
Empathy
Adaptation

THE WHAT

Present a slide deck you've never seen. You know that dream where you're called on to speak about something and you suddenly realize you're utterly unprepared and forgot to get dressed? This is the clothes-on version of that nightmare.

THE HOW

Jump In: With no preparation, each person has to present a ten-slide deck for five complete minutes as if they know what they're talking about. Which they don't. Because they've never seen this deck before. Speakers can control the slides and advance at their own rate. If they are stumped, they can always turn it on the audience and ask, "Who knows what I'm about to say?" When five minutes is up or the deck is finished, the presentation is over, and the speaker introduces the next victim.

Celebrate: No matter how the presenter did, the crowd goes wild.

Breathe: When everyone has had their time in the spotlight, open the floor for comments, and then close out with the why.

THE WHY

"Um. Well. Uh." That is *not* how you want to respond when someone catches you off guard. Thinking on your feet is a muscle. This is a playful workout. Because there's no way to be good at this, everyone just has to lean in and roll with the punches. It's uncomfortable and impossible, and that's the point, so no one has to worry about doing well. Depending on your experience, take stock of what made it torture (fear of being judged, imperfection, desire to please, all eyes on you) or terrific (no consequences, free to create, all eyes on you).

THE MATERIALS

Prepare the decks ahead of time. You can actually buy premade decks online. But if you're going to build your own, here are some pointers:

> *Build the decks around a loose theme.* If the slides are all random, the presenter can't get any momentum. That said, a little randomness is part of the fun. Add a capybara or Victorian illustration midway through and see what they can make of it.
>
> *Keep the slides simple.* Big images, minimal words, and simple charts give the presenter the most runway to work.
>
> *Give it some structure.* Start each deck with a title slide and make it clear when they reach the last slide by numbering the slides—ten slides max.

In-Person Extras:
  A large display for displaying the slides
  A computer that the presenter can use to see and control the slides

KINDA KINTSUGI: MINDFUL MENDING

Primary Quality
Persistence

Supporting Themes
Problem-Solving
Patience
Optimism

THE WHAT

Celebrating the damage. *Kintsugi* is a Japanese art of repair that highlights the repair instead of hiding it. Aside from creating stunning pieces of art, it's a wonderful metaphor for celebrating the damage that comes from living in the world, which shows how the repair can make something even more valuable. The real stuff is repaired with real gold. If that's in your budget, go for it. I used gold-looking epoxy.

THE HOW

Select: Everyone brings in something special to them that is broken or selects something unbroken that speaks to them and breaks it then and there.

Repair: Fit the pieces back together and use the gold epoxy to repair the item. This takes time and patience. Play some music.

Share: Everyone tells the story behind the thing. If it was theirs to begin with, why is it special? How was it broken? Why have they kept it? If it's new, why did they choose it? How did it feel to break it on purpose? Once the story of every piece has been shared, open the floor for comments, then close out with the why.

THE WHY

In a disposable world, taking the time and care to repair something is a lovely moment to share. It's a fun way to try out an art form few of us are versed in, and the end result is always stunning. But as much as I love the way these look in the end, the real treasure is the stories that come out. This is a great way of both surfacing the formative stories behind the people we know and revealing what and how they assign value to the things and people in their lives.

THE MATERIALS

- You can mix mica powder with epoxy or ceramic glue
- Bamboo or wooden skewers for easy application
- Broken china—any vase, plate, bowl, or cup that people wish to repair
- Unbroken china for breaking—I went to a thrift store and emptied a shelf
- Protective gloves
- Sandpaper sheets (approx. 120–180 grit)—optional
- Or just get a premade kintsugi repair kit

KINDNESS ROCKS: SOLID THINKING

Primary Quality
Connection

Supporting Themes
Resilience
Trust
Generosity

THE WHAT

Add a pop of surprise to the world: Paint a rock to celebrate the things we've survived and acknowledge what we've learned.

THE HOW

Reflect: Everyone thinks about a time when a challenge got the better of them and about the words they needed to hear in that moment. Advice. Comfort. Whatever.

Create: Pick a rock that speaks to you and paint it with the words you needed to hear back in that moment. Once the words are in place, cover the rest of the rock in imagery or colors that echo the spirit of the words.

Share: Everyone shares their creations with the group and tells the story behind it. Once everyone has shared, briefly close out with the why, and then send everyone out into the world to place the rock somewhere in plain sight so it can be spotted by a stranger who needs to hear those very words.

THE WHY

It's one thing to share stories of triumph. It's quite another to share moments of failure. But we can own those moments by seeing them from a distance. We're no longer that person, even if it just happened five minutes ago. By wrapping that unpleasant memory in the advice or comfort we now know we needed, we can rehabilitate that moment from a loss to a learn. Then, instead of keeping it to ourselves, we put it out in the world to recognize that we're not alone in facing these challenges and in the hopes that our words will bring joy or a smile to someone else.

THE MATERIALS

Smooth, fist-sized stones, a rainbow of paint pens if possible, acrylic paint and brushes otherwise

MASKING THE DARKNESS: BRINGING SHADOWS TO LIGHT

Primary Quality
Trust

Supporting Themes
Connection
Problem-Solving
Storytelling

THE WHAT

Before Halloween was about scaring up empty calories it was about scaring away the things that haunt us. But rather than ghosts or ghouls, this activity has us facing the scariest thing ever: ourselves.

THE HOW

Reflect: Think of a moment when your shadow came out. A moment when you found your own behavior horrifying. Perhaps it's the moment you snap in traffic and yell, "GET OUT OF THE WAY!" Perhaps it's when you grabbed your whining kid harder than you imagined you ever would. Perhaps it's when you were ten and slipped your grandmother's beautifully designed Chanel perfume bottle into your pocket.

Create: Now you're going to create a mask that evokes that moment.

Literally, metaphorically, however you want. Stole your brother's Halloween candy? Cover the mask in Reese's Pieces. Lost your temper at someone precious to you? Use the red end of the spectrum of paints to re-create the whirlwind of anger. Embrace this person that you both are and are not.

Share: Everyone puts on their mask and recounts the story of its inspiration. When they are done, they take off the mask and set it aside. When everyone has shared, open the floor for comments, then close out with the why.

THE WHY

Ironically, by creating this mask, we are revealing something that's been hidden. The act of trying to express a memory that we'd rather forget forces us to examine it from multiple angles, trying to understand the heart of the moment in order to express it. The creative elements of the mask allow you to defang the memory and take control of the narrative. Some people want to smash them at this point, which I don't prevent, but I think there's more value in respecting and acknowledging the full spectrum of what we're capable of so that we can be alert and aware of how we're showing up. By evoking that dark moment with a mask in a safe and playful context, we're able to confront that shadow, learn from it, and practice separating ourselves from it to leave it to the past.

THE MATERIALS

Blank, genderless cardboard masks

Imagine a kindergarten art room: Pipe cleaners, pom-poms, googly eyes, markers, popsicle sticks, fabrics, felts, mirrors, gem stickers, beads, feathers, string, disposable coffee cups, air-dry clay, balloons, wooden blocks, anything else within reach

Glue guns, scissors, tape, markers

MEMORY FLOSS: RETHINKING WHAT YOU KNOW

Primary Quality
Resilience

Supporting Themes
Releasing Perfectionism
Humility
Community

THE WHAT
Drawing from memory.

THE HOW

Prep: Come up with five iconic cartoon characters that everyone in the group will definitely know.

Fail: Give everyone five minutes to draw one of the characters from memory. *No cheating.* Don't look it up. Don't look at your neighbor's work. Do your best. This is not about artistic talent; this is about memory. Try to get the details down. The shape of the eyes, the cut of the clothes. What makes Sponge Bob "Sponge Bob"? After five minutes compare your renditions (you may now look up this character to gauge accuracy if you so choose). Repeat the process for a total of five characters.

Celebrate: Once you've drawn five characters, pin up or lay out the results on a spectrum from best memory to worst. Marvel at the chasm between what you think you know and what you actually know. Close out with the why.

THE WHY

This activity is a playful way to inoculate people against the paralysis of fear of failure. As the rounds progress, people become accustomed to the experience of reaching for a memory, an idea, an inspiration, and coming up short. But they learn to just dive in. Give it a try. Do their best. They get to practice not freezing up at the threat of imperfection.

The first round is going to be the toughest. It's not uncommon in the first round for people to sigh, throw up their hands, and get annoyed. It's a shock to the ego to realize you don't really know what you think you know.

But that's just the first round. They'll keep failing, but eventually they'll feel more fun than frustration.

THE MATERIALS

Pencils, 4 by 6 blank index cards

MIND MAPS: CHARTING THE INNER LANDSCAPE

Primary Quality
Empathy

Supporting Themes
Connection
Trust
Community

THE WHAT

We all carry around so much more than whatever we're doing in the moment. Whether it's our children while we're at work or work when we're with our children. This activity helps us sort out our priorities while empathizing with the people around us. Collage your brains out.

THE HOW

Brain Dump: Everyone begins with a large page. I like to start with a big diagram of the brain, but you can also let them draw their own self-portrait. They then fill it in with labels, drawings, and collage materials to represent all the things that occupy their mind. However, certain basic labels like "work," "love," and "family" are off-limits. We're looking for more specific descriptions. "Patience for rambling stories from my kids." "Getting my dad's medication right." "Correctly spelling the word 'unnecessary.'" "Remembering Beatles lyrics." Everyone must dig a little deeper to describe what it is that truly holds their attention, focus, and energy.

More: When you think you're done, go back and fill in the empty spaces with more images, more words, more drawings. You can repeat the themes you've already touched on or add new ones. Just fill in the empty.

Share: Everyone walks us through the landscape of their mind, pointing out the major landmarks, sharing the reason things are the size they are, and describing how long they've been carrying these topics around in their head. When everyone has shared, open the floor for comments, then close out with the why.

THE WHY

It's hard to remember how much we're all juggling in the day-to-day. It's even harder to imagine all that our peers are juggling. This exercise is a silly, colorful way to give ourselves serious credit for all the ways that we show up and all the things we balance on our shoulders. It's equally powerful both to get to know the priorities of our colleagues and to build patience and empathy for the layered complexity of their lives outside of—but necessarily influencing—the work environment.

THE MATERIALS

Magazines of all subjects and decades, wrapping paper, old comics, glitter glue, rainbows of markers and paint pens, glue sticks, scissors, large sheets of paper

ORCHESTRA OF OPTIMISM: THE UNSPOKEN MADE AUDIBLE

Primary Quality
Connection

Supporting Themes
Trust
Community
Storytelling

THE WHAT

Wordless storytelling. Communicating an internal process without words forces us to slow down, reflect, and think about ourselves through a new lens. This is the unspoken made audible. I like to ask for no talking during this activity. In fact, I like to print out the instructions on sheets of paper formatted like the old title cards in silent movies and deliver the instructions that way.

THE HOW

Reflect: Participants begin by reflecting on their experience of going from feeling overwhelmed to feeling like they've got this. What is that process like on the inside? Using an empty sheet of paper, everyone begins by translating their process into a line squiggle that represents their journey from blocked to inspired. Is it a zigzag, an arch, a knot, a concentric spiral?

Compose: Then we move from one sense to another. Instead of words, participants will use sound to tell their story. Using found objects in their vicinity, everyone takes twenty minutes to set their squiggle to music. Rattling paper clips, blowing bubbles in water glasses, drumming on trash cans—they are all fair game. Through rhythm, melody, or cacophony, people translate their silent, internal experience of overcoming overwhelm into a piece of music.

Perform: Everyone performs their piece for the group. The group applauds. Once everyone has performed, open the floor for comments, then close out with the why.

THE WHY

Translating experiences between the senses requires breaking away from the mental shorthand that has served us all our lives and leaving those familiar tools behind. This is analogous to what we're asking of ourselves as we explore new ideas and territories—to give up the easy and familiar ways of thinking and stretch into a new frame of mind.

The shared nature of the activity helps everyone to understand the experience of their teammates in a completely new way—to hear both how they experience this process and how they choose to convey it. It's also a gentle but powerful reminder that we should never assume that people's internal processes are the same as our own.

THE MATERIALS

Paper, pens, anything within reach that can make noise

POETIC POWERS: DOUBLE-EDGED WORDS

Primary Quality
Community

Supporting Themes
Optimism
Purpose
Empathy

THE WHAT

Turn a curse into a blessing. It can be hard to get people to say nice things to each other without it sounding cheesy. Rather than giving people a template for kindness, this activity gives them a template for unpleasantness and uses that darkness as fuel for their light.

THE HOW

Listen: Participants begin by listening to a poem. Not just any poem. A poem that was written as a venomous curse—"I Am Rowing," by Henri Michaux. This is a poem that features such humdingers as, "Your armpits reek far and wide of the crypt," "Someone has slobbered on the laugh of your little child," and "Animals drop dead as you pass." Charming.

Flip the Script: We take Michaux's poem as a foundation but then turn it inside out. Everyone is given a few lines of the poem and asked to write its opposite, to turn the curse into a blessing. So, from "I have cursed the streets your step plod through," one might write, "I have cleared the path so you can dance along your way."

Recite: Everyone comes back together in a circle and reads their new lines in order, one after the other. Reassembled, the lines become a collective benediction of kindness, generosity, and empathy that reflects the kind of atmosphere in which we all hope to live and work. When you reach the end, open he floor for comments, then close out with the why.

THE WHY

Many of us find it easier to be kind to other people than to ourselves. We might encourage a colleague to take a break for lunch and recharge, but do so while working right through lunch ourselves. This activity is a forcing function to generate kindness toward ourselves.

Everyone creates a line to add to the collective and gets to feel kind and generous. But at the same time everyone is on the receiving end of all the benevolence being generated by the group. It is a fun and easy way to support each other and help each other with nourishing and supportive sentiments that might otherwise feel too raw and emotional for a work atmosphere. The words of the poem and the silliness of the activity allow for those powerful sentiments to be smuggled in and made welcome.

THE MATERIALS

Give everyone a numbered sheet with four to eight lines of the poem to work with

SEW MANY RULES: COMPLEXITY FROM SIMPLICITY

Primary Quality
Community

Supporting Themes
Unconventional Thinking
Working with Constraints
Unexpected Outcomes

THE WHAT

You're going to use needles, thread, and simple commands to stitch together some beautiful art pieces with everyone following the same instructions… but with different results.

THE HOW

Contribute: Each person begins with a blank index card (or three if you're a small group), a sewing needle, a piece of fabric, and a good amount of thread in a contrasting color. Everyone writes simple instructions for a stitch on the card. For example: stitch three Xs of different sizes; create a dashed line from seven o'clock to twelve o'clock; use a dashed line to form a triangle that overlaps one other line; make a smile.

Distribute: Shuffle and distribute the cards.

Create: Each card is then interpreted by the individual sewer. How big are the Xs? What direction is the triangle? All dealer's choice. Interpret the card as you will, make your stitch, and then pass that card to the right for your neighbor to interpret as they will. Continue until the group has rotated through all the cards.

Step back and marvel at how you all had the same instructions in the same order and yet managed to create such striking, individual creations of your own. Open the floor for comments, then close out with the why.

THE WHY

This activity began life as an unlikely mash-up of Sol LeWitt–style participatory art and the process of computer coding. (Much like in a computer, data is passed from one function [output] to another [input]. Each sewer acts like a programming function, performing a collection of simple directives, just like a multihuman computer.) But in practice it's a way to reflect on the random beauty of generative systems, the difference between active and passive creativity, and the balance between instruction and interpretation.

It's a prime example of generating innovative thought from within the boundaries of certain constraints, of taking the rules and finding your signature way of expressing them.

THE MATERIALS

Index cards, sewing needles, 5-inch fabric squares, 5-inch embroidery hoops, contrasting thread (I like navy fabric with white thread, but you do you)

SLOW DOWN TO SPEED UP: SIESTA FIESTA

Primary Quality
Self-Care

Supporting Themes
Productivity
Community
Trust

THE WHAT

Take a nap. If you're reading this around the middle of the afternoon, you're probably zoning out already. It's not your fault, you're just wired that way. Our hunter-gatherer ancestors passed down a genetic disposition for afternoon dips that we're all powerless to do anything about. Most of my exercises offer ways to refill your energetic well through active play. But that's not the only tack available. Inspired by my daughter's kindergarten class and the myriad articles on the value of resting during the day, this activity is...a nap.

THE HOW

Permission: In a quiet, private space with mats, blankets, stuffed animals, open by explaining the why. This is a particularly childish activity and adults have an easier time playing when they understand the purpose.

Submission: Everyone briefly puts their high expectations for every moment of their day on pause and takes the time to refuel and refresh their engines. Go ahead and snore.

Share: Afterward, use a large stretch of butcher block paper to have everyone sketch out where they went during their time-out and create a map of your collective dreams. After everyone has shared their contribution to the dream map, open the floor for comments.

THE WHY

Your system is designed to be at peak tiredness around 2:00 a.m. and 2:00 p.m. You can fight it with caffeine or the gym, or you can sack out for a twenty-six-minute siesta.

Why twenty-six? Ask a rocket scientist. NASA found that a quick twenty-six-minute nap led to a whopping 35 percent improvement in task performance and a 50 percent improvement in overall alertness. Numbers like that are hard to ignore. NASA's nap culture has even spread to companies like Nike and Google, which now offer "nap pods" so that their people can get the rest they need to do great work.

Thanks to the natural afternoon dip in your circadian rhythm, the ideal timing for your afternoon astronap is between 1:00 and 3:00 p.m., local earth time.

THE MATERIALS

Mats, blankets, pillows, stuffed animals, bedtime storybook (I suggest *You Are Stardust* by Elon Kelsey and Soyeon Kim)

Nice-to-Have: White noise machine

TOWERING INSPIRATION: BUILDING WITH THE MOMENTS THAT BUILT US

Primary Quality
Gratitude

Supporting Themes
Vulnerability
Connection
Empathy

THE WHAT

A sculpture of inspirational words and images. Charles Eames and Ray Eames were designers famous for lots of things, but my personal favorite is a deck of cards. It's the size of a normal deck of playing cards, but with a twist: Each card has six slots cut into it so that it can interlock and be assembled together with others to form freestanding structures of myriad shapes and sizes. This activity poaches the Eames' concept of slotted cards but takes it in a different direction.

THE HOW

Reflect: Everyone thinks of a person in their life whose inspiration was crucial to the person they grew into. Who set them on their present course? Was it the aunt who told them their opinion mattered? The teacher who pushed their curiosity to the next level? The camp counselor who celebrated their creativity?

Create: Everyone gets two blank, giant pieces of cardboard with notches cut into them. They use these to tell the story of this inspiring relationship in two ways—with words on one card, and with an iconic image on the other. For example, some words from this activity have been: "Intersections are beautiful." "Tame the fire inside to light my way." "Creativity can permeate your whole way of being." "Compassion without action is nothing." The images can range from portraits to patterns, lions to landscapes—whatever is the image that pops into your head when you think of that person.

Connect: Everyone tells the story behind the words and images they chose, and then slots their cards together with other cards, and slowly a collective construction will emerge—an interlocking sculpture of creative inspirations. After everyone has shared, open the floor for comments, then close with the why.

THE WHY

This exercise is a sneaky backdoor way of getting people to brag about themselves and for the group to celebrate their community's diversity. By getting a little vulnerable and trusting the group enough to share about the people who made you who you are and their qualities, you also articulate who you've become and what you're proud to offer to the world.

Building the structure is a striking way to remember the multitude of factors that influences and defines people. It could be a giant sculpture in a living room or a small castle on the conference table. Whatever form works best for your situation, it's a nice way to remember the sparks that led us to where we are today and how we might spark others along their path. Seeing the interlocking nature of our priorities and values, growing in space and mass, filling our field of vision, revealing unexpected connections, overlaps, and contradictions helps us gain a deeper understanding of ourselves, our peers, and our community.

THE MATERIALS

Blank slotted cards (if you've got the space available, I order big 2-foot by 3-foot cards, but feel free to work with whatever size cards you prefer)

Colorful markers (I use dot markers, because the ink flow makes it easy to fill up the big cards)

TWINSIES: QUOTIDIAN COMMONALITIES

Primary Quality
Connection

Supporting Themes
Vulnerability
Trust
Community

THE WHAT

Play matchy-matchy. When people work together remotely, there aren't as many opportunities for chitchatting and hitting upon serendipitous commonalities. "You were at that concert too?!" This activity takes advantage of the isolation of work from home (WFH) to connect people.

THE HOW

House Tour: Participants are paired up in breakout rooms. Then they take their partners on a tour of their space to find objects they have most in common—the more unexpected the better. Do we both love this model of lime squeezer? Have the same artist on our walls? Each treasure a blanket our grandmother knitted? Both have books? Good enough.

Compile: From these commonalities, the entire team assembles a list of Oprah's *Our Favorite Things*. A wild collection of images of the things that the group is drawn to, values, cherishes. Each pair also writes a brief statement of recommendation for their common items.

Share: Each pair shares back what they discovered and their thoughts about what they had in common. Open the floor for comments, then close with the why.

THE WHY

It's a small world, after all. By seeking the mundane overlaps, the esoteric commonalities, we do two things at once. On one hand, we are finding common ground, bridges between our distinct lives that may help us connect and form unexpected bonds.

On the other, we are giving someone else a guided tour of what is special to us and why. In a situation when we visit each other's spaces infrequently at best, this is an intimate yet low-stakes way of sharing the details of our day-to-day worlds.

THE MATERIALS

Laptops or phones with video capabilities, collaborative slide deck or digital white board

ACKNOWLEDGMENTS

While writing this book I was lucky enough to be surrounded by kind, brilliant people who were willing to share their talents, time, perspectives, and even homes to help me create something I'm truly proud of.

Thank you—to Njoki Gitahi, Loren Blackman, and Stefan Killen for lending your discerning eyes and expansive imaginations. To Juan Astasio, who proves that humor and humanity are not distractions from serious work—but the heart of it. To the Walshes—John, Marilyn, Jack, Charlie, and Luna—for the space, the kindness, and the countless slices of pizza that kept me going. To Jason Baker, Trevor Tubelle, and Amy Bonsall—your editorial wisdom made these pages stronger, sharper, and more honest. To Lawrence Abrahamson and Mollie West Duffy—for lighting the first spark and urging me to follow it. To Carrie Staller, Alex Gallafent, Emily Hyland, and Greg Perez—your friendship and enthusiasm have carried me farther than you know. To Jad Abumrad, Ryder Carroll, Ingrid Fetell Lee, and Sandy Speicher—for your generosity, insight, encouragement, and overall awesomeness. To Jaidree Braddix—for guiding me through this process with uncommon patience and professionalism. To Diana Ventimiglia—for believing in this idea from the moment it was just a pitch on a page. To Anstice Carroll—for always being there, exactly when it matters most. And to Lara, Quinn, Phoebe, and Zeus—for your love, your inspiration, your wild imaginations, and your (very) occasional quiet.

NOTES

Chapter 1

1. I was originally going to try to salvage a little dignity and just attribute this advice to a "friend," but I promised vulnerability, so you get the full neon turtle.

2. Vivek Murthy, "Work and the Loneliness Epidemic," *Harvard Business Review*, September 26, 2017, https://hbr.org/2017/09/work-and-the-loneliness-epidemic.

3. Murthy, "Work and the Loneliness Epidemic."

4. Gallup, *State of the Global Workplace: 2023 Report* (Gallup, 2023).

5. Gallup, *State of the Global Workplace: 2023 Report*.

6. Gallup, *State of the Global Workplace: 2023 Report*.

7. Gallup, *State of the Global Workplace: 2023 Report*.

8. Gallup, *State of the Global Workplace: 2023 Report*.

9. Gallup, *State of the Global Workplace: 2023 Report*.

10. Murthy, "Work and the Loneliness Epidemic."

11. Andrew J. Oswald, Eugenio Proto, and Daniel Sgroi, "Happiness and Productivity," *Journal of Labor Economics* 33, no. 4 (2015): 789–822.

12. Patrick Bateson and Daniel Nettle, "Playfulness, Ideas, and Creativity: A Survey," *Creativity Research Journal* 26, no. 2 (2014): 219–222.

13. Katherine Karl and Joy Peluchette, "How Does Workplace Fun Impact Employee Perceptions of Customer Service Quality?" *Journal of Leadership & Organizational Studies* 13, no. 2 (2006): 2–13, https://doi.org/10.1177/10717919070130020201.

14. "Playing Up the Benefits of Play at Work," *Association for Psychological Science*, 13 Oct. 2017, https://www.psychologicalscience.org/news/minds-business/playing-up-the-benefits-of-play-at-work.html.

15. M. J. Tews, J. W. Michel, and A. Bartlett, "The Fundamental Role of Workplace Fun in Applicant Attraction," *Journal of Leadership and Organizational Studies* 19, no. 1 (2012): 105–114.

16. Gallup, *State of the American Workplace Report: 2017 Report* (Gallup, 2017).

17. Gallup, *State of the American Workplace Report: 2017 Report*.

18. Kevin J. Eschleman, Jamie Madsen, Gene Alarcon, and Alex Barelka, "Benefiting from Creative Activity: The Positive Relationships Between Creative Activity, Recovery Experiences, and Performance-Related Outcomes," *Journal of Occupational and Organizational Psychology* 87, no. 3 (2014): 579–598, https://doi.org/10.1111/joop.12064.

19. Glassdoor Team, "Workplace Culture Trends: The Key to Attracting Top Talent in 2017" (Glassdoor, 2017). (This article has been archived and has no active link.)

20. Stuart L. Brown, "Consequences of Play Deprivation," *Scholarpedia* 9, no. 5 (2014): 30449, https://nifplay.org/consequences-of-play-deprivation/.

21. Lisa M. Vanderbleek, Edward H. Robinson, Montserrat Casado-Kehoe, and Mark E. Young, "The Relationship Between Play and Couple Satisfaction and Stability," *Family Journal* 19, no. 2 (2011): 132–139.

22. S. Bourg Carter, "The healing power of friendships," *Psychology Today* (2023, April 11). https://www.psychologytoday.com/us/blog/high-octane-women/201105/the-healing-power-of-friendships.

23. L. Rapaport, "Brain games linked to delayed cognitive decline in elderly," *Reuters* (2017, January 31). https://www.reuters.com/article/us-health-aging-mental-stimulation/brain-games-linked-to-delayed-cognitive-decline-in-elderly-idUSKBN15F2PA.

24. René T. Proyer, Fabian Gander, Katja Brauer, and Garry Chick, "Playfulness and Subjective Well-Being: A Longitudinal Study," *PLOS ONE* 18, no. 6 (2023), e0286260, https://journals.plos.org/plosone/article?id=10.1371/journal.pone.0286260.

25. John J. Ratey, "Beyond Fun and Games: Playfulness May Help Combat Depression," *Psychology Today* (2020, August 12), https://www.psychologytoday.com/us/blog/the-athletes-way/202008/beyond-fun-and-games-playfulness-may-help-combat-depression.

26. Kevin J. Eschleman, Jamie Madsen, Gene Alarcon, and Alex Barelka, "Benefiting from Creative Activity: The Positive Relationships Between Creative Activity, Recovery Experiences, and Performance-Related Outcomes," *Journal of Occupational and Organizational Psychology* 87, no. 3 (2014).

27. René T. Proyer, "Playfulness, Subjective Well-Being and Self-Esteem: A Structural Equation Model," *The European Journal of Humour Research* 1,

no. 3 (2014): 1–24, https://europeanjournalofhumour.org/ejhr/article/view/Rene%20Proyer.

Chapter 2

1. Charles Duhigg, "What Google Learned from Its Quest to Build the Perfect Team," *New York Times*, February 25, 2016, https://www.nytimes.com/2016/02/28/magazine/what-google-learned-from-its-quest-to-build-the-perfect-team.html?_r=0.

2. Other key factors for high-performing teams were trust (you can depend on each other), structure and clarity (you know what's expected of you), meaning of work (your efforts are worthwhile), and impact of work (your contribution is important). But their impact is dwarfed by the impact of psychological safety.

3. Laura Delizonna, "High-Performing Teams Need Psychological Safety. Here's How to Create It," *Harvard Business Review*, August 24, 2017, https://hbr.org/2017/08/high-performing-teams-need-psychological-safety-heres-how-to-create-it.

4. Gentle disclaimer: I talk a lot about this company called IDEO. For me, IDEO was a turning point. It opened up many possibilities and perspectives. But it's worth acknowledging that it was not perfect, as no place is. IDEO has gone through a number of different phases over its forty-year history, and I have friends and colleagues whose time at IDEO was less rewarding than mine. Some significantly so. The same questions of diversity, equity, inclusion, respect, and justice that are woven throughout our culture were in play at IDEO as well. People I dearly love and respect have different takes on the IDEO experience. This book is not meant to pretend that IDEO was all good for all people all the time. Rather, it's a distillation of all the good that I learned during my time there and that I have seen bring good to others.

Chapter 4

1. Andrew J. Oswald, Eugenio Proto, and Daniel Sgroi, "Happiness and Productivity," *Journal of Labor Economics* 33, no. 4 (2015): 789–822.

2. Gallup, *State of the Global Workplace: 2023 Report* (Gallup, 2023).

3. S. Lyubomirsky, L. King, and E. Diener, "The Benefits of Frequent Positive Affect: Does Happiness Lead to Success?" *Psychological Bulletin* 131, no. 6 (2005): 803–855.

4. A. Edmans, "28 Years of Stock-Market Data Shows a Link Between Employee Satisfaction and Long-Term Value," *Harvard Business Review*,

March 24, 2016, https://hbr.org/2016/03/28-years-of-stock-market-data-shows-a-link-between-employee-satisfaction-and-long-term-value.

5. Although a higher salary may initially motivate employees, it's been shown that people quickly adapt to that new level, so it rarely maintains their engagement and motivation in the long run.

6. Oswald, Proto, and Sgroi, "Happiness and Productivity," 789–822.

7. Oswald, Proto, and Sgroi, "Happiness and Productivity," 789–822.

8. A. Whitaker, "Productivity in the Season of Joy: Lessons from Merck's Curiosity Report," Merck KGaA Internal Global Study, April 18, 2020, https://www.emdgroup.com/en/company/curiosity/curiosity-report.html.html?ko.

9. H. K. Wong, I. D. Stephen, and D. R. T. Keeble, "The Own-Race Bias for Face Recognition in a Multiracial Society," *Frontiers in Psychology* 11 (2020): 208.

10. K. J. Johnson and B. L. Fredrickson, "'We All Look the Same to Me': Positive Emotions Eliminate the Own-Race Bias in Face Recognition," *Psychological Science* 16, no. 11 (2005): 875–881.

11. Society for Human Resource Management, *Employee Job Satisfaction and Engagement: Revitalizing a Changing Workforce* (Society for Human Resource Management, 2016).

12. Gartner, *Reinventing the Employee Value Proposition: The Human Deal* (Gartner, 2022).

13. Gallup, *State of the Global Workplace: 2023 Report*.

14. Shane McFeely, "Remote Work Statistics: The State of Remote Work," Quantum Workplace, August 31, 2021, https://www.quantumworkplace.com/future-of-work/remote-work-statistics.

15. Gartner, *Reinventing the Employee Value Proposition*.

16. Gautier, Kate, et al., "Research: How Employee Experience Impacts Your Bottom Line," *Harvard Business Review*, March 22, 2022, https://hbr.org/2022/03/research-how-employee-experience-impacts-your-bottom-line.

17. Ingrid Fetell Lee, interview by Ben Swire, January 22, 2024.

Chapter 5

1. Gavin Lamb, "Suleika Jaouad on Writing in the Space Between Stimulus and Response," *Leaky Grammar*, Medium, June 3, 2021, https://medium.com/leakygrammar/suleika-jaouad-on-writing-in-the-space-between-stimulus-and-response-3fa42efeed7b.

2. Ryder Carroll, interview by Ben Swire, January 16, 2024.

3. Michael F. Steger, Hadassah Littman-Ovadia, Michal Miller, Lauren Menger-Ogle, and Sebastiaan Rothmann, "Engaging in Work Even When It Is Meaningless: Positive Affective Disposition and Meaningful Work Interact in Relation to Work Engagement," *Journal of Career Assessment* 21, no. 2 (2013): 348–361.

4. Catherine Bailey and Adrian Madden, "What Makes Work Meaningful—or Meaningless," *MIT Sloan Management Review* 57, no. 4 (2016): 53–61.

5. Patrick L. Hill and Nicholas A. Turiano, "Purpose in Life as a Predictor of Mortality Across Adulthood," *Psychological Science* 25, no. 7 (2014): 1482–1486.

6. Anthony L. Burrow and Patrick L. Hill, "Purpose as a Form of Identity Capital for Positive Youth Adjustment," *Developmental Psychology* 47, no. 4 (2011): 1196–1206.

7. Patricia A. Boyle, Lisa L. Barnes, Aron S. Buchman, and David A. Bennett, "Purpose in Life Is Associated with Mortality Among Community-Dwelling Older Persons," *Psychosomatic Medicine* 71, no. 5 (2009): 574–579.

8. Robert A. Emmons, "Striving for the Sacred: Personal Goals, Life Meaning, and Religion," *Journal of Social Issues* 61, no. 4 (2005): 731–745.

9. Clark Valberg, in conversation with the author, May 10, 2025.

10. Tara Parker-Pope, "Want to Believe in Yourself? 'Mattering' Is Key," *New York Times*, September 27, 2023.

11. Gordon L. Flett, "An Introduction, Review, and Conceptual Analysis of Mattering as an Essential Construct and an Essential Way of Life," *Journal of Psychoeducational Assessment* 40, no. 1 (2021): 3–36, https://journals.sagepub.com/doi/full/10.1177/07342829211057640.

12. Gordon L. Flett, *The Psychology of Mattering: Understanding the Human Need to Be Significant* (Academic Press, 2018).

13. J. P. Tangney, R. S. Miller, L. Flicker, and D. H. Barlow, "Are Shame, Guilt, and Embarrassment Distinct Emotions?" *Journal of Personality and Social Psychology* 70, no. 6 (1996): 1256–1269, https://pubmed.ncbi.nlm.nih.gov/8667166/.

14. Anne Lamott, *Operating Instructions: A Journal of My Son's First Year* (Pantheon Books, 1993).

15. For some of us, our purpose comes parading down Main Street clanging pots and pans. For others of us, it may be more of a quiet whisper hoping to be recognized. Maybe you, too, had a great idea a few years back but have

decided that the moment has passed. But what if your idea just needed a little time to marinate...

16. This is often the best indicator of what will be most helpful to talk about. Just like the exercise you least want to do is probably the one you need the most, the topic you most want to avoid is probably the one that actually means the most to you.

17. Over the years, many—too many—of our participants have shared with me that this is a first for them, to think of these as traits to be proud of.

18. N * (N - 1) / 2.

Chapter 6

1. Leonard E. Read, "I, Pencil: My Family Tree as Told to Leonard E. Read," *The Freeman* 8 (December 1958): 32–37.

2. "Care Counts: Helping Kids Stay in School," Whirlpool, https://www.whirlpool.com/care-counts.html.

3. Jad Abumrad, interview by Ben Swire, January 10, 2024.

4. I've tried it, and it works better on adults than on kids. When I tried it with my kids, they just stared at me and said, "Yeah, that's what I said!" Kids are the best/worst.

5. When he said this, I realized that I had leaned back and looked up to the left to ponder his point. I was physically detaching from the conversation to have space to process and contextualize this unexpected insight. It was marvelous and annoying at the same time to inadvertently demonstrate his point.

Chapter 7

1. Michelle Gielan, "The Financial Upside of Being an Optimist," *Harvard Business Review*, March 12, 2019, https://hbr.org/2019/03/the-financial-upside-of-being-an-optimist.

2. Jim Keenan, "The Proven Predictor of Sales Success Few Are Using," *Forbes*, December 5, 2015, https://forbes.com/sites/jimkeenan/2015/12/05/the-proven-predictor-of-sales-success-few-are-using/?sh=5275bc54ede6.

3. Ron Kaniel, Cade Massey, and David T. Robinson, "The Importance of Being an Optimist: Evidence from Labor Markets," NBER Working Paper No. 16328 (National Bureau of Economic Research, September 2010), www.nber.org/system/files/working_papers/w16328/w16328.pdf.

4. Nelson Mandela, *Long Walk to Freedom* (Little, Brown, 1994/1995), 1154.

5. Carol S. Dweck, "The Perils and Promises of Praise," *Educational Leadership* 65, no. 2 (2007): 34–39.

6. Sandy Speicher, interview by Ben Swire, February 12, 2024.

7. Alix Spiegel, "By Making a Game Out of Rejection, a Man Conquers Fear," *Morning Edition*, NPR, January 16, 2015, https://www.npr.org/sections/health-shots/2015/01/16/377239011/by-making-a-game-out-of-rejection-a-man-conquers-fear.

Chapter 8

1. Heidi K. Gardner, "Performance Pressure as a Double-edged Sword: Enhancing Team Motivation but Undermining the Use of Team Knowledge," *Administrative Science Quarterly* 57, no. 1 (2012): 1–46, https://journals.sagepub.com/doi/abs/10.1177/0001839212446454.

2. Cigna, *Loneliness and the Workplace: 2020 U.S. Report* (Cigna, 2020).

3. A. Czeszumski, S. H.-Y. Liang, S. Dikker, P. König, C.-P. Lee, S. L. Koole, and B. Kelsen, "Cooperative Behavior Evokes Interbrain Synchrony in the Prefrontal and Temporoparietal Cortex: A Systematic Review and Meta-Analysis of fNIRS Hyperscanning Studies," *eNeuro* 9, no. 2 (2022), https://doi.org/10.1523/ENEURO.0268-21.2022.

4. "How Having a Best Friend at Work Transforms the Workplace," Gallup, October 16, 2018, https://www.gallup.com/cliftonstrengths/en/249605/having-best-friend-work-transforms-workplace.aspx.

5. Emma Seppala, "Connectedness and Health: The Science of Social Connection," Stanford Medicine, May 8, 2014, https://ccare.stanford.edu/uncategorized/connectedness-health-the-science-of-social-connection-infographic/.

Chapter 9

1. Julianne Holt-Lunstad, Timothy B. Smith, and J. Bradley Layton, "Social Relationships and Mortality Risk: A Meta-Analytic Review," *PLOS Medicine*, July 27, 2010, https://journals.plos.org/plosmedicine/article?id=10.1371/journal.pmed.1000316.

2. Vivek Murthy, "Work and the Loneliness Epidemic," *Harvard Business Review*, September 26, 2017, https://hbr.org/2017/09/work-and-the-loneliness-epidemic.

3. Murthy, "Work and the Loneliness Epidemic."

4. Murthy, "Work and the Loneliness Epidemic."

5. Arthur Conan Doyle, "The Boscombe Valley Mystery," in *The Adventures of Sherlock Holmes* (George Newnes, 1892).

6. André Gide, *Le traité du Narcisse* (Perrin et Cie, 1891).

7. Murthy, "Work and the Loneliness Epidemic."

8. Gartner, *Reinventing the Employee Value Proposition: The Human Deal* (Gartner, 2022).

Chapter 10

1. *NeuroArts Blueprint: Advancing the Science of Arts, Health, and Wellbeing* (Aspen Institute, Johns Hopkins School of Medicine, and Center for Applied NeuroAesthetics, 2019), https://neuroartsblueprint.org/wp-content/uploads/2021/11/NeuroArtsBlue_ExSumReport_FinalOnline_spreads_v32.pdf; and Marcus Herdener, Fabrizio Esposito, Francesco di Salle, Christian Boller, Caroline C. Hilti, Benedikt Habermeyer, Klaus Scheffler, Stephan Wetzel, Erich Seifritz, and Katja Cattapan-Ludewig, "Musical Training Induces Functional Plasticity in Human Hippocampus," *Journal of Neuroscience* 30, no. 4 (2010): 1377–1384, https://www.ncbi.nlm.nih.gov/pmc/articles/PMC3842475/.

Chapter 11

1. Oversimplified summaries: Human-centered research means talking with people about their needs and behaviors. Rapid prototyping means testing out half-baked ideas to quickly gather insights for the final design.

ABOUT THE AUTHOR

Ben Swire is one of today's most innovative thought leaders on company culture and workplace belonging. An award-winning designer, writer, and former Design Lead at the iconic innovation firm IDEO, Swire cofounded Make Believe Works, a team-building company that uses creative activities to accelerate connection, deepen trust, and fuel collaboration. His methods have helped organizations from Fortune 500 companies to public school districts build healthy and productive workplace cultures. He lives in Brooklyn, New York.

RAISING READERS
Books Build Bright Futures

Thank you for reading this book and for being a reader of books in general. As an author, I am so grateful to share being part of a community of readers with you, and I hope you will join me in passing our love of books on to the next generation of readers.

Did you know that reading for enjoyment is the single biggest predictor of a child's future happiness and success?

More than family circumstances, parents' educational background, or income, reading impacts a child's future academic performance, emotional well-being, communication skills, economic security, ambition, and happiness.

Studies show that kids reading for enjoyment in the US is in rapid decline:

- In 2012, 53% of 9-year-olds read almost every day. Just 10 years later, in 2022, the number had fallen to 39%.
- In 2012, 27% of 13-year-olds read for fun daily. By 2023, that number was just 14%.

Together, we can commit to **Raising Readers** and change this trend. How?

- Read to children in your life daily.
- Model reading as a fun activity.
- Reduce screen time.
- Start a family, school, or community book club.
- Visit bookstores and libraries regularly.
- Listen to audiobooks.
- Read the book before you see the movie.
- Encourage your child to read aloud to a pet or stuffed animal.
- Give books as gifts.
- Donate books to families and communities in need.

Books build bright futures, and **Raising Readers** is our shared responsibility.

For more information, visit **JoinRaisingReaders.com**

Sources: National Endowment for the Arts, National Assessment of Educational Progress, WorldBookDay.org, Nielsen BookData's 2023 "Understanding the Children's Book Consumer"